The Pubs
of
Hereford City

The Pubs
of
Hereford City

by
Ron Shoesmith

Logaston Press

LOGASTON PRESS
Little Logaston Woonton Almeley
Herefordshire HR3 6QH

First published by Logaston Press 1994
Copyright © Ron Shoesmith 1994

ISBN 1 873827 14 8

Set in Times 11/13 pt by Logaston Press
and printed in Great Britain
by Ebenezer Baylis & Son, Worcester

This book is dedicated to the memory of Dick Vowles
who was City Councillor, past Mayor of Hereford,
Chairman of the City of Hereford Archaeology Committee,
and personal friend.
He took an active interest in this project from its inception
and had made a start in preparing the information
for publication shortly before he died.

During the first half of the 19th century it was the custom to have an official 'news reader' in several Hereford taverns. A London paper, delivered by stagecoach, and the local Hereford newspapers would be read aloud and discussed. The atmosphere was far more that of a gentleman's club than a public house and seats were only available to the more eminent of the local tradesmen, often by election. The original oak-panelled room with its armed seating, in which the news was read, still survives in the Bunch of Grapes Tavern in Hereford and the atmosphere of this historic inn at that time has been captured in this drawing by Brian Byron.

Contents

Acknowledgements

In September 1985, a Manpower Services Commission archaeology project was established jointly by Hereford City Council and the City of Hereford Archaeology Committee. Up to twenty people were involved in the several major excavations and building surveys which followed. Documentary research was one of the many facets of the programme and one result was a well-catalogued collection of over two hundred files containing information about the inns and taverns of Hereford. The participants in the scheme, who were responsible for gathering this information together, are too many to mention individually, but without their work this book would never have been published. They were supervised by Alan Thomas who, together with Julie Phillips, put a considerable amount of time and effort into the project.

In the 1950's the *Hereford Citizen and Bulletin* ran a series of articles on Hereford inns and signs by Mr. Evans which provided much of the background for this research. A lot of the information which followed was obtained from documentary sources such as the reports of the licensing justices and from early newspapers. The staff of the Hereford branches of the County Library and the Record Office, and especially Robin Hill and Sue Hubbard, have helped throughout with unfailing good humour and deserve my most grateful thanks.

My employers, the City of Hereford Archaeology Committee, allowed me to make use of the information in their files; Anne Sandford, of the City Museum, and Derek Foxton provided many of the photographs; Ken Hoverd, the honorary photographer to the Archaeology Unit, copied the older photographs and provided present-day ones where necessary; Brian Byron, the Illustrator to the Unit, produced the maps and the frontpiece—without all their help this would have been a much less interesting book.

Following a request in the columns of the *Hereford Times*, a large number of people phoned or wrote to me with information about various inns, both open and closed. Special mention should be made of Mrs. Gittings, Mr. Wilce, Mr. Tanner and an un-named gentleman from Abergavveny, who were all of particular help. I have made use of this material wherever possible and would like to acknowledge with my most grateful thanks, the help that they have provided.

My wife and two children have tolerated me throughout the production of this book, and have suffered my worries as the final date arrived without it being fully complete. This also meant much burning of midnight candles from Andy Johnson of Logaston Press. My apologies to them all for my slowness and my thanks for their kindnesses and understanding.

The sources of many of the illustrations used in this book are as follows:

Hereford City Museums: pp. 6, 15, 49, 57, 60, 66, 67, 69, 83, 85, 88, 92, 93, 99, 104, 105, 130, 151, 156, 176, 192, 206.

Hereford City Council: pp. 139, 144, 146, 149, 150, 154.

Hereford County Library: pp. 26, 114, 138.

Derek Foxton: pp. 39, 43, 47, 62, 86, 113, 115, 121, 129, 162, 202, 208.

Ken Hoverd: pp 13, 33, 56, 76, 106, 171, 174 (lower), 196.

City of Hereford Archaeology Committee: pp. 148, 153, 183 (upper), 188.

Mrs. Gittings: pp. 78, 117.

Hereford Record Office: pp. 29.

Introduction

The roadside inn, the large town centre hotel, the old-established tavern and the street corner public house are all particularly British institutions that have grown through the ages both as a matter of need and as a result of a complex series of Acts of Parliament. For many centuries they have provided the opportunity for people of all classes to meet, to drink, to eat, and particularly to talk. They have provided accommodation, sometimes good and sometimes poor, for the traveller and his steed, be it a horse or latterly a car. They have provided entertainment—from bear baiting and cock fighting to billiards and bowls. They have provided food, from the simple ploughman's to full à la carte menus. They comprise many of our most historic buildings, for the wholesale rebuilding of licensed premises came only with difficulty and after much pressure.

No attempt has been made in this book to include all the information available about the inns and taverns of Hereford. Such a work would be of almost encyclopaedic length, for the information available in the official records, in newspapers and by word of mouth, is immense. The main danger in writing this book has always been that it would end up as long lists of names; not just of licensed premises, both open and long-closed, but of all the men and women who were the licensees. Every effort has been made to avoid this pitfall, but in the presentation there has had to be a degree of organisation of the information to ensure that the record is reasonably complete.

The easiest method of presentation would have been to produce an alphabetical list, but this would have had little attraction and would inevitably have been boring to the reader. An alternative approach has been chosen which, it is hoped, will provide more general interest and be more readable. The first chapter consists of a basic history—an attempt to show how the British inn came about, what it served and how, as a result of varying legislation, it has changed through the ages. The second chapter deals with the most important product of our inns—the cider, ale and beer—where it was made and how it was produced. The fourteen remaining chapters each cover a distinct area of the city. One covers the central area of High Town; then three chapters deal with the old Saxon town. This is followed by a further four chapters which describe the inns, past and present, within the rest of the walled city. The losses due to the construction of the Inner Relief Road have a chapter to themselves while each of the five remaining chapters describes one of the suburbs within the city boundaries.

Ron Shoesmith
November 1994

CHAPTER ONE

ALEHOUSES, TAVERNS AND INNS

The first roads in this country which were laid out on a formal basis were made during the 350 year period when the Britain was just within the frontier of the Roman Empire. Travellers using these roads would have needed places where they could get accommodation and food—alcoholic refreshments would doubtless have been available to those who required them. The Romans imported wine from other parts of the Empire and made every effort to grow vines in the southern part of England. They would also have made mead, possibly cider, and as wheat and barley were both available, some form of ale.

The nearest Roman settlement to Hereford was the walled town of Magnis, near Kenchester and some 5 miles to the west of the city. This had been built on the edge of the Roman military area which covered the whole of Wales. With its broad main street and large public buildings it would, without any doubt, have had guest houses providing overnight accommodation and houses in which soldiers returning from a stint in Wales could drink and enjoy themselves.

During the early Roman occupation of this area, before their engineers had constructed a bridge across the Wye near Magnis, the main road, built by the army to join the legionary fortresses of Chester and Caerleon, probably crossed the river at one of the Hereford fords. Then, and possibly throughout much of the Roman period, there is likely to have been a roadside house close to the ford which would have provided a boat for a dry crossing and refreshment and accommodation for travellers should the river be in flood.

1

After the end of the Roman Empire, it is unlikely that there was any settlement in the immediate area of Hereford before the 7th century when the diocese was created, apart from the religious establishment of St. Guthlac which may have been founded at a slightly earlier date. Once a cathedral had been built on the gravel terrace overlooking the ford across the river, a small settlement would have grown outside the religous precinct. The city's first inns, as simple drinking houses, could well date to this period. Indeed, as early as 750A.D., the then Archbishop of York issued a Canon 'That no priest go to eat or drink in taverns', and there were so many inns by the time of King Edgar (959-75) that he issued a decree limiting their number to one per village.

By the beginning of the ninth century Hereford was a well-established small town with its own defences against possible incursions by the Welsh and the Vikings. By the time of the Norman Conquest, it had become one of the most important towns in the country largely because of its important strategical position on the Welsh border. By then a substantial defensive work enclosed the Saxon town and its cathedral. The rapid growth of the city outside the old defences, which took place immediately after the Conquest, would inevitably have resulted in an increase in the number of inns and taverns.

Associated with this growth came various measures to limit the numbers of drinking houses and to protect the customer. One of the most important of these was the 'Assize of Bread and Ale' in 1266. This enactment accepted the principle that both bread and ale were necessities for all people in the country and, for a period of some three hundred years, it ensured that the retail price of ale was fixed according to the price of grain. At that time, ale was usually made from malted barley, or occasionally wheat, steeped in water and fermented with yeast.

During the 13th century there was a gradual increase in the sale of wine, and a separation came into being between 'taverns', which sold both ale and wine, and 'alehouses' which sold only ale. In addition there were the inns or 'hostels' that provided accommodation as well as food and drink.

In Hereford, according to Richard Johnson in his *Ancient Customs of the City of Hereford*, it was an offence, in conformity with an old Saxon custom, to 'lodge any person more than one day and one night against whom the slightest suspicion existed without speedily informing the mayor, and upon default become liable to a fine of twenty pence.' Apparently the city beadle had the job of making 'diligent search in the houses of those suspected of harbouring vagrants, idle persons, or strange beggars, and to bring such before the mayor; they were then examined as to their doings, way of living, and dwelling-place, and if they gave an unsatisfactory account of themselves they were expelled from the city or sentenced to be whipped at the "cart tail", which punishment on these occasions was executed by the beadle.'

During the medieval period the principal hospitality for travellers was still provided by the monasteries—it was only along the more important pilgrim routes that guest houses and wayside inns were established and these would have been well beyond the purse of all except the richest of travellers. However, a gradual change occurred and during the 14th and 15th centuries, as the influence of the church started to wane and merchants began to travel, wayside inns became a feature of the countryside and hotels providing accommodation and food began to appear in the market towns.

For perhaps a thousand years ale had been the basic drink throughout the country but here too a fundamental change occurred during the early 15th century. This was due to the introduction of hops, described at the time by the authorities in Shrewsbury as that 'wicked and pernicious weed', and the resultant manufacture of 'beer'. The hops gave the new drink a more bitter flavour and was of considerable importance for its preservative properties. For well over a hundred years brewers produced both ale and beer, but the popularity of the former gradually declined and beer eventually became the national drink. It was not until towards the end of the 17th century that there was any serious competition whatsoever to ale and beer in the retail market. Even then, the cost of coffee and tea for the next half-a-century or more was prohibitively expensive for all but the richer classes.

The first licensing law came at the end of the 15th century. It empowered justices of the peace to close alehouses and to obtain sureties for good behaviour from the landlords and, if necessary, to close alehouses. Fifty years later they obtained the power, which

3

they still retain, to both licence and suppress alehouses—hence 'licensed premises'.

A year later, in 1553, came an Act which limited the number of 'taverns', and thus the sale of wine—London was allowed forty; York, nine; Bristol, six; whilst Hereford was limited to three, along with places such as Lincoln, Worcester, Southampton and Oxford. The Act also prohibited the sale of French wines. This did not mean that the population of the country were being deprived of places in which to drink—there were approximately forty-four alehouses for every tavern in the latter part of the 16th century, equivalent to more than one drinking establishment for every two hundred persons, a far higher ratio than exists today.

Previously, there must have been quite a few more taverns in Hereford than was allowed by this new law and as a result there were several instances of citizens getting into trouble. In one case William Hill was brought before the Mayor 'for selling and putting for sale certain kinds of wine contrary to the form of the statute'. Mr. Hill was a freeman of the city and was committed to the Booth-hall, which was the freeman's prison, 'there to remain during master mayor's pleasure'. However, he did not stay there and it was eventually agreed that he should be 'disenfranchised and thence-forth accounted a foreigner and no freeman or free merchant'. Perhaps there should have been more sympathy for Mr. Hill's case than was shown, especially when it is appreciated that the Mayor at that time was a John Kerry, who also owned a tavern which was on the list to be closed. There is no indication of what happened to William Hill, but John Kerry's ingenious solution to his own problem is described in a later chapter.

These early alehouses were probably little different to the timber-framed and thatched houses which surrounded them. The larger ones would have had sheds at the rear where brewing was carried out and possible cellars in which to store their brew at a constant temperature.

The taverns, being of a higher status and including sales of wine as well as ale and beer, were probably of a superior construction. With this in mind it is worth noting that the more important of the towns and cities in the country tend to be well-endowed with substantial stone cellars of late medieval date. These often had well-constructed vaulted roofs and entries from the streets which were obviously designed for public use. Were these the buildings that were used as taverns or higher-class ale-houses in the 15th and 16th centuries? In Hereford, the cellars underneath what was the Greyhound Hotel, next to All Saints Church and, a little further to the east, those under the more-recently closed **Pippin** may well be cases in point. Others, such as those which still exist on the south side of High Town and underneath the **Spread Eagle** in King Street, could have served a similar purpose.

Throughout most of recorded history it was a legal requirement that all drinking establisments should be identified by a sign. Poles, which gradually became longer and heavier, had the sign suspended from them. In the case of a tavern, there would also be an evergreen bush, which represented the vine and indicated that wine was for sale. Alfred Watkins, in an article in the *Transactions of the Woolhope Naturalists' Field Club*, also mentions a 'chequers' sign, which was apparently common in Hereford and elsewhere. It consisted of alternate diamonds or lozenges of green and red painted on the frames on each side of the entrance to the inn. He suggested that the sign originated in the counting board (like a chess board, but used for counting money) and that it was an indication that the innkeeper kept such a board for the benefit of his customers. He discovered one at the **New Harp** (before it was rebuilt) and another associated with the **Booth Hall**.

Various attempts were made during the Civil War to levy duty on both the manufacture and the sale of beer and ale—attempts which were consolidated after the war and are still in force. By this time beer was of three qualities: strong, table, and small, and each variety attracted a different rate of duty. It was not until the late 19th century that the duty levied became based on the original gravity of the beer.

Although there was a duty on beer, spirits were exempt and towards the end of the 17th century and into the 18th there was what Monckton in his *History of the English Public House* described as 'one of the biggest orgies of over-indulgence our island history has ever seen'. Every small alehouse in the country was in a position to sell cheap brandy and in particular, gin. The result was that consumption of spirits increased from half-a-million

The Railway Inn in Barton Road, later to become the Antelope

gallons in 1684 to over eight million gallons in 1743—well over one
gallon per person per annum! The various Gin Acts that followed
together with increased duties and a strengthening of the powers of
the justices, rapidly changed this trend and by 1758 excise duty was
paid on less than two million gallons. The 'gin era' was over.

The regulation of the public house continued to attract government interest and from 1729 licence renewal had to be made at annual Brewster Sessions, originally in September then, at a later date, in February.

Before the beginning of the 17th century inns were providing food for travellers and accommodation, often in rooms laid out around galleried courtyards. By the 18th century most of these establishments had lost their earlier reputation for being rat-infested hovels and were becoming orderly and well-equipped. However, there was still room for improvement as Viscount Torrington's experiences around 1790 show—'I look upon an inn, as the seat of all roguery, profaness, and debauchery; and sicken of them every day, by hearing nothing but oaths, and abuse of each other, and brutality to horses ... all town inns are so noisy by low company and intemperance'.

However, James Boswell in his *Life of Samuel Johnson* gives a totally different picture. 'There is no private house,' said Johnson, talking on this subject, 'in which people can enjoy themselves so well as at a capital tavern. ... The master of the house is anxious to entertain his guests; the guests are anxious to be agreeable to him; and no man but a very impudent dog indeed can as freely command what is in another's house as if it were his own. Whereas, at a tavern, there is a general freedom from anxiety. You are sure you are welcome; and the more noise you make, the more trouble you give, the more good things you call for, the welcomer you are. No servants will attend you with the alacrity which waiters do, who are incited by the prospect of an immediate reward in proportion as they please. No, sir, there is nothing which has yet been contrived by man, by which so much happiness is produced, as by a good tavern or inn.'

The early 19th century was the culmination of coach travel and inns were at the height of their prosperity. They had an enviable reputation which is well expressed by Washington Irving in *Travelling at Christmas*: 'As we drove into the great gateway of the inn, I saw on one side the light of a rousing kitchen fire beaming through a window. I entered, and admired for the hundredth time, that picture of convenience, neatness, and broad honest enjoyment, the kitchen of an English inn. It was of spacious dimensions; hung

St. Peter's Street: The recently closed David Garrick with its heavy pediments, and the remains of the timber-framed Sun, now T. Lloyd Davies' chemist shop

round by copper and tin vessels, highly polished, and decorated here and there with a Christmas green. Hams, tongues, and flitches of bacon, were suspended from the ceiling; a smoke-jack made its ceaseless clanking beside the fireplace, and a clock ticked in one corner. A well scoured deal table extended along one side of the kitchen, with a cold round of beef, and other hearty viands upon it, over which two foaming tankards of ale seemed mounting guard. Travellers of inferior orders were preparing to attack this stout repast, while others sat smoking or gossiping over their ale, on two high-backed oaken settles beside the fire. Trim housemaids were hurrying backwards and forwards under the directions of a fresh, bustling landlady; but still seizing an occasional moment to exchange a flippant word, and have a rallying laugh with the group round the fire.'

It was during the 19th century that most of the legislation which affects the present-day consumption and sale of alcoholic drink was enacted. The Alehouse Act of 1828 meant that the licensee no longer had to find sureties for his behaviour. However, he was bound to use the legal, stamped measures, not to adulterate his drinks, and not to permit drunkenness on his premises. The Beerhouse Acts of 1830, 1834 and 1840 followed—the first allowed premises to open for the sale of beer, but not spirits, on payment of a simple excise licence; the second differentiated between 'on' and 'off' licences and made 'on' licences more difficult to obtain; whilst the third ensured that licences were issued only to the occupier of the premises. Throughout the country as a whole there was a proliferation of beer-houses following the first Act, although only a few were opened in Hereford.

At that time there were few restrictions on licensing hours. As a whole, the only non-permitted hours were during Divine Services on Sundays, Christmas Day or Good Friday. Beer houses could only open between 4 a.m. and 10 p.m. The 1872 Licensing Act tidied up and tightened the complex legislation, but at the beginning of the 20th century public houses were, in general, still allowed to open for some twenty hours each day.

Towards the end of the 19th century and in the early years of the present century, considerable efforts were made to close down inns by refusing the renewal of licences and by paying compensation to the owners and landlords. In Hereford, by 1919, the Compensation Authority had approved the closure of no less than 35 public houses at a cost of some £16,000.

It is often not realised that the regulations concerning children are mainly of the present century. Although the 1872 Act made it an offence to sell spirits to those using licensed premises under the age of sixteen, it was not until the Children's Act of 1908 that children under the age of fourteen were prohibited in licensed premises. In 1923 it became, in general, an offence to serve alcoholic drinks to those under eighteen.

Regulations brought in at a time of war often have a habit of staying. It was during the First World War that limited opening hours were instigated—in Hereford this meant that closing time was 9 p.m.! The Licensing Act of 1921 regularised this situation by defining 'permitted hours' as being eight hours between 11 a.m. and 10 p.m. except Sunday which was limited to five hours. In 1934, an extension could be granted to 10.30 p.m. during the summer months and especially in rural areas where evening work was necessary.

After the Second World War there were several minor Acts which culminated in that of 1961 which provided for 'restaurant' and 'residential' licences. It also gave the customers' grace—the ten minutes of 'drinking-up time'. A more recent Act has restored the situation to more or less what it was at the beginning of the century by allowing inns to stay open throughout the day if they so wish.

CHAPTER TWO

BREWING AND BREWERIES

When Daniel Defoe passed through Herefordshire at the beginning of the 18th century he noted that the populace were 'diligent and laborious people, chiefly addicted to husbandry, and they boast, perhaps, not without reason, that they have the finest wool, the best hops, and the richest cyder in all Britain'. As far as cider was concerned, he went on to say 'here it was, that several times for 20 miles together, we could get no beer or ale in their publick houses, only cyder; and that so very good, so fine, and so cheap, that we never found fault with the exchange; great quantities of this cyder are sent to London, even by land carriage tho' so very remote, which is an evidence for the goodness of it, beyond contradiction.' The importance was that cider and ale were both safe drinks at a time when most water supplies were at the best suspect and often could cause serious illnesses.

Until relatively recently cider was made on almost every farm in Herefordshire. It was sometimes produced as a cash crop, but was usually made by the farm labourers for their own needs, once the harvest was in. It was made from special cider apples, which are rather unpleasant to the taste as they contain a lot of tannin. Such apples are rich in sugar and, as the farm cider was produced without yeast, it was fully fermented to become a still, acidic drink, invigorating and thirst-quenching during the heat of summer hay-making.

Late in the 19th and during the first half of the 20th centuries, cider was made by several firms in Hereford including W. Evans and Co., H. Godwin & Son, and H.P. Bulmer & Co. Bulmer's was founded in 1887 and by 1888 had moved to premises in Maylord

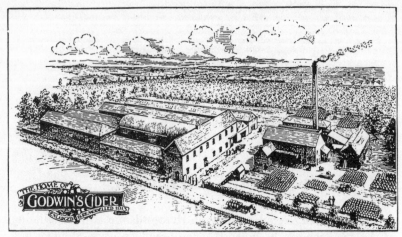

The cider works at Holmer of H. Godwin & Son in 1915

Street. They eventually centralised their operations in Ryelands Street and, more recently, in Plough Lane. They are now the largest cider producers in the country. Godwin & Son had premises at Holmer, where their factory was enlarged and remodelled in 1913, but they have been closed for many years. Evans & Co. had their works on Widemarsh Common. They continued to produce cider in Hereford until well after the end of the Second World War, but eventually closed and the buildings were all demolished by 1975.

Until the middle of the 19th century most landlords made their own ale and beer in small brewhouses behind their inns. Few of these survive today—they have either been demolished or converted to become part of the main buildings of the inn. One that remains recognisably as a brewery building is at the rear of what was the **Sun Inn** in St. Peter's Street, now a chemists shop. It can be seen from the corner of East Street and Offa Street. However, many of the smaller inns and beer-houses that opened during the first half of the 19th century had no brewing facilities whatsoever and were totally dependent on other inns or on the growing number of breweries for their supply. This change continued to accelerate as breweries started to buy public houses as they came onto the market, a process which resulted in a substantial decrease in the number of 'free houses'. This was followed by a series of mergers and takeovers until only a few of the largest breweries survived.

The brewery at the rear of the old Sun in St. Peter's Street

The change was so great that, by the beginning of the Second World War, only two pubs in Hereford—the **Sawyers Rest** and the **Crown**—were brewing their own beer and, not surprisingly, both were beer-houses. By the end of the war, the tradition of inns producing their own beer had completely ceased in Hereford.

The first brewery of any size that was built in Hereford was the one belonging to J.C. Reynolds. He had originally started in business at Fownhope, but moved to a new site in Hereford in 1834 where he established himself as a brewer, maltster and wine and spirit merchant. He may have started this type of business a few years too early for a provincial town such as Hereford, for he had a total lack of success and the brewery was closed for about 12 years.

The Hereford Brewery, shortly after it opened

In 1845 the whole establishment was bought by Charles Watkins, who had previously been the landlord of the **Three Crowns** in Eign Street and then of the **Imperial Inn** in Widemarsh Street. Watkins had previously brewed his own beer in a small brew-house at the rear of the **Imperial**, but this new acquisition enabled him to put his creative energy to work in increasing output and in finding new sales outlets. He started his new business by adopting an eagle as his trade mark and by changing the name of the firm from the Hereford Brewery to the much more imposing Imperial Brewery, capitalising on the name of the inn he owned in Widemarsh Street.

Within a few years he was producing 'Imperial Household and Pale Ales', described as 'pure and sound, and unrivalled for excellence of quality and value combined'. Mild and bitter beers were available at one shilling a gallon and pale ale at 1s. 2d. and all were supplied in 9, 18, 36 and 54 gallon casks, delivered free. He was also responsible for the well-named Golden Sunlight Pale Ale which won a gold medal at an International Exhibition in 1886 and became a 'best-seller' for the firm.

Inside the Hereford Brewery
—circular and square fermenting vessels

The brewery grew rapidly and with the profits Charles Watkins was able to buy or lease several public houses both in Hereford and in the surrounding areas. He then had the outlets in which he could sell the beer he was brewing in increasing quantities. By 1870, the brewery had been so successful that Watkins was able to buy the adjoining Bewell House and extend the brewery yard first through to Wall Street and then to Newmarket Street. In 1876 he expanded again, buying the redundant Iron and Brass Foundry in Friar Street and converting it to become the Imperial Flour Mills and Maltings. He also grew his own hops and farmed at Marden, Holmer and Burghill.

However, the brewery was still the centre of the Watkins family enterprises and eventually Henry, the eldest son, was taken into partnership. Unfortunately, Charles and his son, Henry, both died in 1889 and the Imperial empire was then managed by Charles' two other sons, Charles and Alfred. Neither of the two brothers was particularly interested in the brewing trade and they appointed Henry James Hull as Manager and Head Brewer and provided him with accommodation at Bewell House. The brewery continued to expand and by the mid-1890's was one of the major businesses in Hereford, having reverted to its original name—the Hereford Brewery.

In its heyday at the end of the 19th century the main brewery buildings were arranged on both sides of the private road which led from Bewell Street through to Wall Street. On the right was the vat room with a beer cellar underneath and further in, a large, partially covered area which was used for washing and storing casks. On the other side of the road was the wine and spirit stores, also with cellars; the brewery with its fermenting and racking rooms, and further cask storage and cleansing areas. Smaller buildings included the cooper's shop, the wheelwright's shop, stables and harness rooms. On the western side of Mr. Hull's house there was the beer stores with, in front of it and facing Bewell Street, the Monarch Mineral Water Factory that had started its life as St. George's Hall—an ice skating rink—yet another of Charles Watkins enterprises!

The quality of the many products from the brewery was said to be due to the water used in all the processes, which came from the famous Bewell Spring by means of an artesian well some 40ft. deep. It had been discovered in 1724 and had always 'yielded an unfailing supply of excellent brewing liquor'.

This was the part of the family business that the two Watkins brothers decided to put on the market in 1898 as they were 'desirous of retiring'. Included in the sale was the brewery with its plant and all the other buildings on the site; 35 hotels, public houses and beer houses in the city and neighbourhood; and branches in Birmingham, Cardiff and Swansea. It also included the various trademarks including the famous Golden Sunlight. It is not surprising, considering the size of the business, that the sale was held in London. The City Library copy of the sale particulars is marked '£64,000 highest bid for the lot'.

The brewery was acquired by the Tredegar Brewery Company and a name change followed, the new firm becoming the Hereford and Tredegar Brewery Co. The Hereford base became their main production centre in 1906 when they closed their Brecon and Tredegar breweries. The supply of water was a growing problem, but the situation was resolved when a local diviner found an additional water supply some 88 ft. deep, which was described as being 'of crystal clearness and purity'. By this time the Watkins' manager, Mr. Hull, had left, to go to the **Sun Tavern** in St. Peter's Street where he became landlord and brewer. He was probably responsible for building the new brewery that still survives at the rear of the building. The new manager of the Hereford Brewery was Arnold Daly Briscoe who stayed with the company until well into the 1930's. By 1950 change was in the air as a result of a merger which established a new firm: the Hereford, Tredegar and Cheltenham Brewery.

These changes were also to affect the other main brewing works in Hereford, which had been founded during the latter part of the 19th century. This was the City Brewery situated on the south side of Maylord Street. Here, Arnold, Perrett & Co. had their brewery and works, having purchased the main part of the property from Robert William Miller in 1890. The site was very limited as compared with that of the Hereford Brewery, but it was sufficiently large to be able to produce all the necessary beer for consumption in the gradually-growing number of inns belonging to the company in the Hereford area. To accommodate their lorries and dray horses, the company also obtained an area in Maylord Street that had been a blacksmith's shop. Arnold, Perrett & Co. were eventually associated with the Stroud Brewery and in 1924, a Trust Deed transferred the ownership of the whole of the Maylord Street premises to the Cheltenham Original Brewery Co. Ltd.

An additional area, which consisted of a row of six cottages at the rear of 15 Commercial Street, was bought by the Cheltenham Original Brewery Co. in 1937. These cottages were called nos. 5-10 Brewer's Terrace. This name was nothing at all to do with the adjoining brewery—it was because the previous owner's family had the surname Brewer! These tenements were demolished probably before the Second World War to make way for additional brewery buildings. Brewer's Passage, which originally led from Commercial Street to these cottages, still exists and now provides one of the pedestrian routes into Maylord Orchards.

The city brewery firm was eventually amalgamated with the Hereford Brewery in Bewell Street and the joint firm then became the Cheltenham and Hereford Breweries Ltd. although they continued to make use of the trade names such as the Tredegar Brewery, the Stroud Brewery and Arnold Perrett & Co. for parts of their various enterprises. Brewing continued in Maylord Street until May 1948 after which the site was just used for storage and distribution. It was eventually offered for sale in 1951 because the firm was concentrating all their brewing operations in the city 'at their other extensive premises in Bewell Street'. To protect their interests, the brewery company insisted on a restrictive covenant prohibiting the purchaser and his successors from carrying out any production, supply or distribution of spirits, wine, beer, porter, cider or perry on or from the premises. The purchase price was £7,600 and the whole area is now within the Maylord Orchards development.

Following the acquisition of the Cheltenham and Hereford Brewery by Whitbreads, brewing operations ceased in the Bewell Street works. After a few years as a distribution centre all the buildings on the site were demolished in the early 1960's apart from Bewell House. A small part of the area then disappeared underneath the Relief Road, but the remainder was used as an open car park for many years until the Tesco supermarket was built on the site.

Following this closure there was a period of some thirty years when beer for public consumption was no longer produced in Hereford. Indeed, beer brewed at individual inns throughout the country almost ceased, with only a few notable examples such as the Three Tuns at Bishop's Castle surviving. Convenience beers, in pressurised barrels that did not depend on the skill of the landlord, flooded the market. For a time, it looked as though the old-fashioned beer-engine, used to draw the beer up from the carefully-racked barrels in the cellars, would be a thing of the past. A welcome change has occurred in recent years and locally produced beer is again available. The Wye Valley Brewery, based at the **Barrels Inn** in St. Owen Street, now has its beer in many local inns. 'Specialist beers'—the products of the many smaller breweries that have opened throughout the country—are available in many pubs, and the beer-engine has made its welcome return on most bar counters.

CHAPTER THREE

THE HIGH TOWN AREA

High Town was originally part of the western approach to the magnificent market place designed by William fitzOsbern, Earl of Hereford, directly after the Norman Conquest in order to attract French settlers to his new territory. The main part of the market consisted of not just High Town, but the whole of the triangular area between Commercial Street, Union Street, and St. Peter's Street. To the south was the three-hundred year old Saxon town surrounding the cathedral and enclosed within the defensive line of a ditch, a wall and an embankment. By designing his new town outside the northern defences of the Saxon settlement, fitzOsbern expressed his complete lack of interest in the early town. He emphasised his contempt for the original inhabitants by deliberately building his new church of All Saints directly outside the old North Gate.

This grand market place was approached by new, wide roads—Commercial Road leading from the north-east, St. Owen Street from the south-east, and Eign Gate Street and Bewell Street, then together as one street, forming the route from the west. Widemarsh Street, the highway from the north, was then and remains now a narrow road, for it was in use before fitzOsbern's time leading into the old Saxon town. As they arrived, the French settlers would have been provided with strips of land laid out parallel to each other along the sides of the access roads and around the market place. These 'burgage' plots were rapidly taken up, for fitzOsbern provided the new settlers with what was basically a tax advantage over the original residents by allowing them to 'have all their forfei-

19

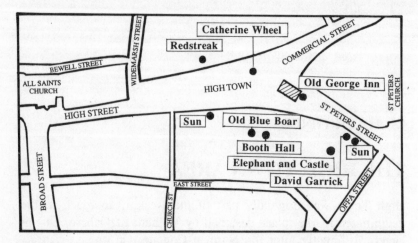

tures discharged for 12d.' (apart from breach of the peace, house-breaking and highway robbery). This inducement, which is described in detail in the Domesday Survey, ensured that the new town of Hereford was an unqualified success. The Saxons, restricted within their old, cramped town, must have viewed the spacious market place with its new shops and houses with some envy. To obtain access, apart from through the North Gate at the end of Broad Street, they had to construct paths across the disused defences—such paths were probably little more that a scramble over the embankment and a plank bridge across the ditch—but these routes were to survive for over nine hundred years as the narrow part of Church Street, the Booth Hall Passage, Barroll Street, and the recently-widened Offa Street.

Within a short space of time all the central plots had been taken up and newer settlers would have been allowed to develop the old defensive area between High Town and East Street, levelling the embankment and filling the ditch to provide level plots.

As time went on the flimsy stalls, which would originally have filled the market place, were converted to more permanent structures. Eventually, living accommodation would have been added on upper floors and gradually the open triangular area became full of buildings. High Town suffered the same fate—it is only within the last two hundred years that such 'nuisances' (as they were called) were demolished.

The burgage plots around High Town, the new plots created on top of the old defensive works, and the market infilling, were where the most important shops and eventually the principal inns and taverns of the growing city were built. In recent years High Town has continued to attract traders who are willing to pay high rents and gradually the public houses have been bought out and converted to shops and offices to the extent that there are now no longer any inns facing this large open space.

As far as has been established there was only one inn on the north side of High Town—the **Redstreak** Inn, or, as it was earlier known, the **Redstreak Tree** Inn. This was doubtless named after the famous cider apple developed by the first Viscount Scudamore on his Holme Lacy estate near Hereford before the Civil War. Of the redstreak, Worlidge said it 'was to be preferred for your Plantation to any other apple whatsoever, especially remote from your House. First, because it yields the best of British Drinks. Secondly, because the fruit is harsh and unpleasant, not tempting the Palates of lewd Persons'.

Was it from the **Redstreak** Inn in 1609 that twelve men danced a Morris Dance in High Town, their combined ages making over twelve hundred years? 'For what some wanted of 100 years, others exceeded ... and all were reported to be constant cider drinkers.' The earliest mention of the **Redstreak** was the sale in 1740 of 'A freehold new (re)built house situated at the Guildhall, with large courts, a large summer house, a large garden well planted with fruit trees, large stables and coach house and all convenience fit for a gentleman, now used as a Tavern in the occupation of Thomas Ford.'

Apparently the **Redstreak** had the narrow frontage to High Town which is now occupied by the Butter Market entrance. At the rear the plot widened and continued through to Maylord Street, where there was a coach entrance. In 1775, the **Redstreak** was the starting point for the first coach to undertake a twice-weekly journey from Hereford to London. 'Pruen's Flying Machine' started at seven in the morning and took thirty-six hours for the journey.

The **Redstreak** was one of the principal inns in the city in the late 18th century and, amongst other entertainments, cock-fighting was a regular event. In 1771, there was a match between the Gentlemen of Herefordshire and the Gentlemen of Radnorshire.

21

Such matches had high stakes and it would appear that Hereford was a centre for the 'sport'.

The **New Inn** in Widemarsh Street had grounds which adjoined those of the **Redstreak**, and in 1809 both were bought by the Corporation to provide land on which to build a Council Chamber, a Guildhall, and a poultry and butter market. The **Redstreak** was demolished to provide the entry to the market from High Town. The Butter Market was completed in 1816, but was open to the heavens, not being covered in for some forty years. The **Redstreak** in High Town had completely disappeared, but the house name was to return at a later date attached to a property in Maylord Street.

In the middle of High Town, the three-storey Market Hall or Guildhall, which stood on twenty-seven wooden pillars, was an imposing sight to all visitors to Hereford. It was demolished in 'a memorable piece of municipal vandalism' in 1862 (to quote Pevsner in his *Buildings of England: Herefordshire*). The Market Hall stood between the **Redstreak** Inn on the north and another inn called the **Sun Tavern** on the southern side of High Town.

The **Sun** in High Town has long been closed, but was once of considerable importance and was apparently where the Royalists tended to gather during the Civil War. In the 1730's the tavern also acted as the Post Office until that function was moved to the **City Arms**. A century later, in 1839, when Fanny Wild was relinquishing the premises, she held a farewell dinner which was announced in the *Hereford Times*. After soliciting the attendance of her 'Agricultural friends and the Public generally' she informs them that dinner will be on the table at two o'clock and that 'Tickets (are) to be had at the bar, 10s. each, including Dessert and a Bottle of Wine.' She was followed as licensee by several members of the Allen family who ran the inn until it closed in 1860. This closure was apparently anticipated, for in April 1859 there was an announcement that 'consequent upon the approaching demolition of the old **Sun** Tavern in High Town, the Victoria Lodge of Odd Fellows, M. U., have moved to the **Kerry Arms**.'

The replacement building, number 25 High Town, still survives and was for many years the home of George Mason's grocery business. After a spell as an International Store it is now part of W. H. Smith's.

To save confusion, the nearby **Sun** Tavern in St. Peter's Street is the next to be described. Curley did not show it on his plan made in 1858 (displayed in the rear passage of the Town Hall) and it probably replaced the High Town **Sun** following the latter's demolition. The landlord for many years, Thomas Bach Ingram, was also a cutler—one wonders if he sold knives along with his alcoholic wares! An interesting reminder of this rather short-lived inn is at the rear and visible from East Street. This is the brewhouse, built of brick by the new landlord, Henry James Hull, in 1903. Although it has lost all the brewing equipment which must have been inside, there have been few external changes and it remains a fine industrial building of its period.

The new **Sun** survived well into the twentieth century, but time was eventually called in 1925. The building, with part of its historic timber frame exposed on the side elevation, still survives as T. Lloyd Davies' chemist shop, between the now closed and boarded-up **David Garrick** Inn and the Trustee Savings Bank.

The **David Garrick** was for many years called simply the **Garrick Hotel**, but when first opened it was called the **Gardeners Arms**. It is not shown as an inn on the 1858 map of the city, but, as it is mentioned in the Directory for that year, it was presumably being built. The building has a rusticated ground floor and a neo-classical facade including over-heavy triangular pediments to the first-floor windows. Garrick, the actor, after whom the hotel was named, was born at the **Angel Inn** in Widemarsh Street in 1717.

In 1870 the **Garrick Hotel** was sold by auction and was then described as being 'in one of the best positions for business in the city.' The main building 'which was rebuilt some years ago by the owner and occupier ... as a Public House contained a well-fitted bar, with side entrance, smoke room, kitchen, back kitchen and yard.' There was a sitting-room and two bedrooms on the first floor and three more bedrooms on the second floor. This was a modern building for its day for it had water closets 'up and down stairs and gas and water are laid on.' At the rear was a malt house and brewery where 'a considerable retail cask trade in Home Brewed Beer has been carried on in addition to the ordinary business of an Inn.' It was a popular house with touring companies playing at the Garrick Theatre and with staff on the *Hereford Journal*.

By 1917, it was owned by Thomas Salt & Co. Ltd., Brewers of Burton-on-Trent. In January of that year, Mr. Scobie, the Clerk to the City Justices, wrote to inform them that the licensee, a Mrs. Matthews, was convicted on the 20th January 'for permitting the consumption of intoxicating liquor to take place after 9 p.m. contrary to the Order of the Central Control Board.' The fine was two pounds and the Brewery replied expressing their sorrow and asking Mr. Scobie if 'the magistrates will expect us to get a fresh tenant?' Mr. Scobie in his reply commented that 'There is no general objection to women licensees at present' (Mr. Scobie's underline!) and went on to say that it was up to the police to object to an individual. He also pointed out that there was another conviction in the Register under the Defence of the Realm Regulations. This was in 1916 when Mrs. Matthews had been fined £10 with a guinea costs for 'selling intoxicating liquor to members of His Majesty's Forces undergoing Hospital Treatment!'

In more recent years the **Garrick** had somewhat of a reputation with the younger generation when the back bar became the Ulu Bar—the first 'theme' pub in Hereford! It is very much a pity that this, the only inn left in the immediate High Town area, has been closed and boarded up for so long.

Only two doors from the **Garrick** towards the main part of High Town was the **Elephant and Castle**. Dunkling & Wright in their *Pub Names of Britain* explain that the sign was derived from the crest of the Cutlers' Company, used by them since 1622. This is an elephant with, on its back, a howdah looking just like a miniature castle. The elephant was probably on the crest because knife handles were often made of ivory. This is far more likely than the ingenious suggestion that the name derives from 'Infanta de Castile'.

The **Elephant & Castle** was a long, narrow building which stretched back two-thirds of the way to East Street and had been an inn since at least the 18th century and possibly earlier. In 1837 it was described as an 'old-established Inn ... containing eight bedrooms, several closets, bar, two parlours, two kitchens, and extensive cellaring, with a brewhouse, malthouse, stables etc'. The sale description also mentions that 'there are two pews in St. Peter's Church belonging to the premises.' However, in 1847, James

24

Matthews proudly advertised that the premises had been 'wholly rebuilt'. Almost, but not completely, for he kept at least part of the original cellarage. The dressed stone cellar, with its four-centred vaulted roof, still survives underneath number 19, now Keith and Peter's.

James Matthews supplied families with 'Best London Gin sold from 10s. to 14s. per gallon; Rum at 15s. per gallon' whilst real French Brandy cost 24s. (or the very best at 26s.) per gallon.

By 1886 the front part of the building had been converted to a shop, but the **Elephant and Castle** continued to survive with an access down a narrow passage. It was then entered in the Street Directories of the period as number 10½ St. Peter's Street. The **Elephant and Castle** was one of the many inns closed by the Licensing Committee in the early part of the twentieth century. Compensation of £305 was paid to the owner and a mere £45 to the licensee. It was closed on the 3rd January, 1917. At that time the Licensing Committee had extinguished 33 licences at a total cost of £15,550.

In 1955 the building was the headquarters of the British Legion; it is now a licensed premises once again, but as a night club rather than an inn.

It is only a short step along High Town from the narrow passage which once led to the **Elephant and Castle** to the equally narrow passage which still leads to the **Booth Hall Hotel** and from there through to East Street. It was in 1392 that Henry Catchepolle sold to Thomas Chippenham and two others a tenement called 'Bothehall'. Some six months later, the mayor and commonalty of Hereford obtained a licence from the king to acquire this building and grounds. Thomas Chippenham was one of the principal citizens of the city being mayor in 1390 and again from 1397 to 1399. He must have been far-sighted in his purchases, for it was in this area that the municipal and merchant guild buildings were erected, well before the construction of the Guildhall and Market Hall in the middle of High Town.

The earliest building was probably the Booth Hall, built about 1400. Its antiquity was appreciated in 1876, when a writer in the *Hereford Times* noted that 'although a great portion is very old I understand it has been well kept and in good repair.' The writer

Part of the late fourteenth century Booth Hall (Alfred Watkins)

goes on to recollect that in his youth 'many times hearing of a ghost that was said to have haunted it, and that it was positively laid by a visitation of dignitaries of the Cathedral and other clergymen and pious people and sundry laymen, several of whom were somewhat of the wag genus. I have heard the late facetious "Tom Cooke" describe the event, but I have now forgotten the particulars.'

For many years the precise whereabouts of the Booth Hall itself was unknown—it was only rediscovered in 1919 when a chimney stack fell, exposing the magnificent medieval roof. This is some 45ft. long and consists of six bays with alternate tie-beam and hammer-beam trusses. The hammer-beams include figures of angels facing downwards, whilst cusped windbraces form arches and quatrefoils in the roof. It was built as a first-floor hall and although the whole of the ground floor is now completely lost it may well have consisted of an open area with the upper floor supported on pillars. Indeed, the Booth Hall Passage, which was a much wider driving-way in the 18th century, goes directly underneath the Hall. The Booth Hall was apparently used by the Mercers Guild for its meetings and for wholesale trade in woollen goods and, later, tanned leather. A building at the rear of the Hall and adjoining East Street was used for many years as the Freemen's Prison—a more salubrious place for the well-to-do offender that the city gaol in Bye Street Gate!

The date when the **Booth Hall** first became an inn is uncertain, but in 1686 Thomas Parry, a painter, declared that 'Hee was at the Cockpitt att Peter Seabornes house called the **Booth Hall** seeing a cockfitting'. A Joseph Gwillim applied for an alehouse licence in 1727 and again in 1735, so the Booth Hall must already have been an inn by that time. In 1783 George Willim (presumably Joseph's grandson) was allowed to buy the whole property from the Council providing he rebuilt the front to High Town 'in a handsome and ornamental manner'. Willim's building (numbers 18 and 19 High Town) still stands although it has had many alterations.

For many years the historic Hall has not been the main part of the inn; this was the 18th century range of buildings which continued from the Hall through to East Street. On the ground floor was a market room, warehousing and stables, but above, stretching through the present first and second floors, was a rather fine Assembly Room. It has long been converted into two floors each containing a series of small rooms, but there are still fragments of the ceiling mouldings and pilasters which belonged to this large chamber, which must have seen many well-attended social events during the 19th century.

In the early years of that century the **Booth Hall** had a notable landlord. This was Thomas Winter Spring, who was born at Fownhope and achieved fame as the champion barefist fighter of all England. He won the title in eight rounds and defended it twice. The defence was not so easy—the first match ran for 75 rounds and the second needed 77 rounds. Spring advertised his farewell dinner at the **Booth Hall** in 1827.

Adjoining the **Booth Hall** there was for some time another tavern, the **Old Blue Boar**. This was described in a late 18th century deed as being to the west of the **Booth Hall** and to the south of the street 'where the fishboards used to stand'. The fishboards, tables on which fish were sold, were apparently in that area of High Town which adjoined the entrance to the Booth Hall Passage. The **Old Blue Boar** could date back to the time of the

Wars of the Roses—the struggle between the houses of Lancaster and York for the throne of England. The White Boar was a heraldic reference to Richard III, killed at the Battle of Bosworth in 1485. The Blue Boar was the symbol of the Earl of Oxford, a supporter of Henry Tudor, who was crowned Henry VII at the scene of the battle. It was doubtless then that many white boars became blue overnight.

The **Old Blue Boar** must have been fairly large for it stretched all the way through from High Town to East Street. An early mention of it was in an advertisement in 1727 which offered for sale 'Twenty couples of good Harriers or Fox-hounds in the hands of a servant. Enquire Mr. Edward Davies at the **Blue Boar**, Hereford.' Although this was apparently one of the most important inns in the city during the 18th century, by 1803 the rear part had been divided into two tenements with the front part being shops facing onto High Town.

This should have been the end of the story, but the building which had been used as the **Old Blue Boar** continued to have a fascinating history. In the early 19th century the whole property belonged to a William Bennett, but he sold it to Augustus Charles Edwards in 1869. A successful draper, Augustus Edwards eventually expanded from the building which was then called Alban House into the adjoining property in front of the **Booth Hall**. He created what he proudly called the ladies' emporium of Hereford— a successful business which was to continue for many years. In 1934, the firm needed more room and demolished the 16th century timber-framed building in the rear yard to make way for a new extension. It appeared that all traces of the **Old Blue Boar** had finally disappeared, but this was not the case.

A few years ago Alban House fell empty following Mothercare's move to new premises in Maylord Orchards. By this time the building was in need of comprehensive refurbishment and it was completely stripped out. As modern timberwork and plasterboard were removed, two bays of an early 16th century building were exposed—the remaining part of the building which, it was supposed, had been completely demolished in 1934. A rapid examination demonstrated that this had originally been an imposing, jettied building some 60ft. long, which had faced the **Booth Hall** across a small courtyard. The high, moulded and panelled ceiling of the ground floor suggests that it was designed as a large hall rather than a series of rooms, although there were separate rooms upstairs. Was this the Guildhall which we know from documentary sources was built in 1490? Was it eventually converted to become the **Old Blue Boar** when the new Market Hall was built in High Town in the late 16th century? The remains are certainly part of the **Blue Boar** and, as a result of sympathetic restoration, this small part of the historic inn can once again be appreciated in both the ground and first floors of River Island, the clothes shop which has now taken over Alban House.

Apart from the **Redstreak Tree** and the early **Sun** Tavern, traces of the other inns which were once around High Town can still be seen, but there are two where the buildings have completely disappeared—the **Old George** Inn and the **Catherine Wheel**.

In the 18th century and for many years before, the eastern part of High Town contained two rows of houses, Butchers Row and Cooken Row. The Old House is the sole survivor of these two Rows and originally had timber-framed buildings attached to both sides. One part of Butchers Row filled the middle of St. Peter's Street, but the main part ran from the Old House into High Town with its buildings facing south, whilst Cooken Row ran back-to-back to Butchers Row thus facing north. The building on the east of the Old House was the **Old George** which spent its declining years as a butcher's shop.

The Old House with the Old George to the right (Wathen, 1798)

29

In 1796, John Price in his *Historical Account of the City of Hereford* described Butchers Row as 'the one encroachment upon the regularity of Hereford, which every man of public spirit ought to contribute something towards removing'. This was partly as a result of the 1774 Parliamentary Act which set up Commissioners responsible for 'Paving, Cleansing, and Lighting the Streets of Hereford, and removing Nuisances and Annoyances therein'. This was the Act under which the City Gates had been removed and on the 18th July, 1815, the Minute Book records: 'The old house at the south end of the Butcher Row, formerly an Inn, the **Old George**, having been purchased by the Commissioners for the purpose of widening the street, it is ordered that the deficiency of the purchase money be paid out of the rates.'

Cooken Row, which was separated from the Old House by a narrow passage called Golden Alley, continued into the centre of High Town. Here the bakers and confectioners plied their trade with the **Catherine Wheel** at the centre. This was one of several **Catherine Wheel's** which, from time to time, could be found in the streets of Hereford. The spiked wheel, on which St. Catherine of Alexandria was martyred, was the badge of the Knights of St. Catherine of Mount Sinai. They protected pilgrims on their way to Jerusalem and the general use of this sign in the Middle Ages probably refers to the protection and care of travellers which could be expected from the inn.

In 1694-5, within living memory of the Civil War, this particular **Catherine Wheel** was kept by a Bridget Andrews, who, like most citizens of Hereford, was a Jacobite. The Corporation manuscripts record that 'Divers persons disaffected ... do weekly and daily resort there and read private, false and seditious news-letters to corrupt his Majesty's subjects'. The inevitable happened when a soldier in the alehouse rashly drank the health of William III. The resultant riot involved the landlady, her daughters, servants and customers who all attacked the soldiers. Within five days of the incident the inn was closed. The building survived for a considerable time with different uses, but by 1837 all the buildings in Butchers Row and Cooken Row, with the exception of the Old House, had been demolished.

CHAPTER FOUR

THE OLD TOWN:
THE BROAD, MAIN STREET

From High Town, the narrow High Street leads westwards towards All Saints, the church originally built by William fitzOsbern outside the North Gate of the Saxon city. Until the Norman Conquest and probably for some time thereafter, it was here that Broad Street was sealed with a gatehouse and a bridge crossing a defensive ditch. Indeed, this part of Broad Street remained narrow until the end of the 18th century when the large building on the eastern side, now Barclays Bank, was built as a town house for the Duke of Norfolk. It was constructed on top of the soft fill of the Saxon ditch; subsidence occurred, and the slight slope of the cills of the windows on each side of the main doorway reflects the 1000 year old defences which are buried underneath.

Broad Street was one of the two main streets of the Saxon city. From the North Gate it would have led originally in an almost straight line, through the present entry to the Bishop's Palace grounds, to a ford across the river Wye. One of the main reasons for positioning Hereford here and indeed, for its name, was the presence of two good fords across the river. The wide part of Broad Street now terminates at the junction with King Street, although the alignment is continued with the narrow Palace Yard. On the edge of the Cathedral Close, facing King Street, there used to be a row of Georgian buildings. Under threat as early as 1837, these buildings were eventually demolished in 1935, partly to provide an open view towards the cathedral. The remainder of the Close is still surrounded by the large houses once occupied by the cathedral

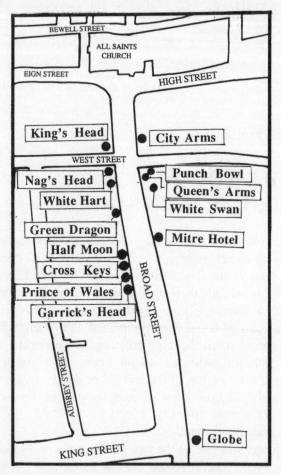

dignitaries. During the Saxon period, when the cathedral would have been smaller and to the south of its present position, King Street probably continued across the Close to join up with Castle Street. This would then have formed the main west-east road of the early city.

William Collins, writing in 1915, said of Broad Street:

'We are impressed as we pass along with its wide pavements, numerous banks, and still more numerous hotels with garages. The bold Doric front of the Roman Catholic Church, dedicated to St. Francis Xavier, is imposing. Adjoining the church is the Post Office, and two doors higher the entrance to Cathedral Close. On the opposite side is the Corn Exchange and hard by the Public Library and Museum erected in 1874'.

Many changes have occurred since Collins wrote his *Historical Landmarks of Hereford* and the western side of Broad Street has suffered more than most. On the King Street, Broad Street corner, the house which had been used by the Canon residentiary during the late 19th century and later became a private hotel called The Residence, has made way for a flat-topped office block. The library and museum building, with stone animals climbing over the facade, is a pleasant 19th century survivor, but the early 1960's office blocks to the north provide a poor substitute for the Corn Exchange which was built in 1857 and eventually incorporated the Kemble Theatre. This building, with its impressive clock tower, and all the surrounding shops, were demolished in 1963.

Broad Street, at the beginning of the 20th century, was indeed a street of banks and hotels, expressing the city's importance as the financial and cultural centre of Herefordshire. The banks are still there, but only two hotels survive, the small **Queen's Arms** on the corner with East Street, and the amalgamation of buildings behind a majestic facade that is now the **Green Dragon** Hotel.

The Queen's, with the timber-framed ex-Punch Bowl to the side

But this description of public houses must have some order, and the east side of Broad Street will be dealt with first. A brief mention has already been made of Barclays Bank—until relatively recently the **City Arms Hotel**—but the story starts at a much earlier date. It was when this part of Broad Street was still a narrow passage, reflecting the early gateway, that the predecessor of the hotel, called the **Swan and Falcon**, was an important Coaching and Posting inn. As early as 1549, Richard ap Rise was the landlord of the **Fawcon** in Brode Street, presumably the same establishment. By the time of the Civil War it had become the **Swan and Falcon** with various members of the Jones' family as licensees. In 1655 there was a pump at this end of Broad Street described as being near the '**Focken** (Falcon) doore'.

During the 18th century inns often arranged entertainments for local citizens. Thus in 1748:

'By the Warwickshire Company of Comedians, at the **Swan and Falcon** at Hereford, on Monday evening being the 26th December will be acted a comedy, called: "A Bold Stroke for a Wife, or the Quaker Outwitted". To which will be added, a pantomime entertainment, called "Harlequins Nuptials". To begin exactly at 6 o'clock.'

A suggestion was made at a meeting of the Common Council in August 1787 that the Commissioners 'purchase and take down the North Gate in a line with Broad Street, and to open the same, the pass through being at present a great nuisance'. The Council were even prepared to subscribe £100 towards the cost.

However, the problem was resolved in 1790 when the inn was bought by Charles Howard, 11th Duke of Norfolk, following his election as Chief Steward of the City. Election of 'one famous and discreet man' to this honorary post had been granted to the citizens of Hereford by James I in 1620. Charles Howard, who had married Frances Scudamore of Holme Lacy in 1771, had quite a reputation. Humfrys, in his *Memories of Hereford*, recounts how an old Clerk 'had seen the Duke astride a barrel of beer in the High Town of Hereford, distributing beer during the progress of an election, and his own condition can easily be imagined!' Perhaps his appetite for alcoholic drink was one of the reasons that Howard rebuilt the **Swan and Falcon** with the intention of making use of it as a Town House as well as an inn.

The new front was set back to line up with the rest of Broad Street and on July 9th, 1793, 'the Great Room at the **Swan and Falcon Inn** in the City, which has been built on a very extensive and most convenient plan, was for the first time opened for the reception of company, with a public dinner to which upwards of 100 people sat down. The meeting was honoured by the presence of the Duke of Norfolk and many other neighbouring gentlemen'.

The 'Great Room', which was on the first floor, was some 70 feet long and 28 feet high—there was nothing comparable in the city. On the ground floor there were four large parlours, a coffee room, a bar, a housekeeper's room and other conveniences. By 1795, the **Swan and Falcon** had become the **City Arms**, but the new name did not impress and it was often called the **Hotel Inn** or simply the **Hotel**. During the 19th century the **City Arms** was perhaps the most important of the city's coaching inns. It was from here that the Royal Mail coaches and the fast but expensive Light Coaches travelled to various parts of the country. In the 1830's the licensee of this successful inn was Thomas Brookes.

The inn was for sale by auction in 1841, following the death of John Bosley. There must have been some uncertainty about its future for the details mention 'The great facility with which the property can be divided into lots suitable for shops or private residences must be seen, and its situation cannot be excelled for all the purposes trade may require.' It continued as an inn, and in April, 1843, Mr. Braham was 'honoured to announce that he, and his son and pupil, Mr. Charles Braham, would give a concert, sacred and miscellaneous, in the Assembly Room.' Tickets were 4s. and 'books of words', 6d.

The arrival of the railways from Newport, Shrewsbury, Gloucester, Worcester and eventually Brecon in the 1850's and '60's ended the coaching era, and was disastrous to the trade of the **City Arms**. In 1866, to balance the books, the northern part of the establishment was sold to the Gloucestershire Bank for a little over £2,000. The Gloucestershire was eventually absorbed by the Midland Bank and the reconstructed northern building is now a branch of Burtons, spoiling what would otherwise have been a superb, balanced, Georgian facade.

The railways were not entirely a bad thing for the historic coaching inns of the city, for they eventually brought visitors and commercial representatives in ever increasing numbers. In 1892, the landlord of the **City Arms**, Thomas Clutterbuck, was able to say that he 'makes it his constant aim that his guests, at least, shall miss as little as may be the comforts of home'. By 1898, the establishment was ready to expand and a four-storey block containing some 20 additional bedrooms and facing onto West Street (as this section of East Street was then confusingly called!) was erected. It was very popular with commercial travellers who brought their stock in huge wicker hampers which were transported from Barrs Court Station by the hotel's own private horse-drawn omnibus and 'trailer'.

The **City Arms Hotel** continued to provide good and reliable service through the first half of the 20th century and was much used by American servicemen based at Foxley during the Second World War. It eventually became part of the Trust House Group along with the **Green Dragon** opposite. However, a long-term problem was beginning to manifest itself. The foundations had been laid on the mud of the long-abandoned Saxon city ditch and, although extensive renovation work had been carried out in 1939, the building once again started to move and the hotel was eventually closed. In 1973, planning permission was granted for it to be converted to a branch of Barclays Bank, conditional on the retention of the Georgian facade. The front and side walls were carefully shored and scaffolded and all the internal floors and walls were

Demolition of The City Arms showing the retained facade

then removed. In effect, a new building was constructed within the shell of the old **City Arms**.

Barclays Bank seems a long cry from the timber-framed **Swan and Falcon** which once graced the North Gate area of Broad Street, but surprisingly not all has been lost. Hidden inside the rear part of the bank and totally invisible to the general public, is a remnant of that early building which has now survived two demolitions. Described by Jim Tonkin as a late 15th or early 16th century town house, this building originally consisted of a first-floor hall or great chamber with moulded purlins and two arch-braced, collar-beam trusses. Perhaps, during one of the future renovations to the bank, this link with the early history of the site can be properly exposed to public view.

Across what is now East Street, but in earlier times was Packers Lane, the **Queen's Arms** could at one time have been overshadowed by its larger northern neighbour. However, it has survived all its competitors to become the last tavern in Broad Street—one could hardly call the **Green Dragon** a tavern! **The Queen's** is a curious building, which from Broad Street appears to be early Victorian, but from the narrow East Street has timber-framed elements which continue into the bar area. The explanation is relatively simple—at the turn of the century the present establishment was no less than three separate buildings. The right-hand part of the Broad Street frontage was a one-room fruiterer's shop, the left part was the **Queen's**, whilst the timber-framed section facing onto East Street was a totally separate inn called the **Punch Bowl**. Punch was originally a sailors' drink which became popular in the seventeenth century. It usually consists of wine or spirits mixed with hot water or milk, sugar, lemons and spices and was always made in a large bowl, hence the inn name.

This must have been one of the smallest of the Hereford inns, measuring just 28 feet long by 13 feet wide. The ground floor included a tiny bar and a separate smoke room, both with corner fireplaces and separated by flights of stairs leading down to the cellars and up to the two, small, first-floor bedrooms. To add to the general confusion the **Punch Bowl** was officially numbered 8 West Street, for the change from West to East then occurred at the junction with Church Street and not, as one would expect, at Broad Street. At that time the **Queen's Arms** consisted of one front room that contained the bar, and a long passage which led behind the **Punch Bowl** to the smoke room at the rear.

The **Punch Bowl** was swallowed up by its slightly larger neighbour in 1901. Most of the internal walls at ground-floor level have since been whittled away and the doorway which once led into East Street has long been blocked. The small shop in Broad Street had a longer history and functioned as a newsagent's for many years. It is only recently that it was amalgamated into the inn.

Almost all records seem to have been lost of the **White Swan** in Broad Street, but it was apparently noted for its strong beer. This may well have been the **Swan Inn** mentioned by John Price in his late eighteenth century *Historical Account of the City of Hereford*.

He found an epitaph in the cathedral graveyard to one Benjamin Thomas 'who was of a festive and joyous humour, and spent much of his time at the **Swan Inn**'. It read:

> Oft at the Swan has BEN kill'd time,
> 'Mong sons of mirth - a venial crime -
> But, strange! old Time revives! - What then?
> Time, in revenge, has now kill'd BEN.

The **White Swan** was let in October 1778 to a Thomas Harper, who was previously at the **Globe Tavern** in the same street, and continued in use till the mid 1850's. An Elizabethan half-timbered building, it was demolished in 1864 to make way for the National Provincial Bank.

The Mitre Hotel in its heyday

Two doors lower down the street was the much more famous **Mitre Hotel**, one of the main coaching inns of the early 19th century. The mitre is the tall cap, deeply cleft at the top, worn by bishops as a symbol of their office and has been a common name for inns in cathedral cities since the fifteenth century. Dr. Johnson, Boswell, Goldsmith and their friends used to meet in London at The Mitre in Fleet Street.

In 1738 the **Mitre** included facilities for housing and weighing hops, and by 1807 the Hereford Clerical Society was meeting there. In 1812, it was the meeting place of the oddly-named 'Silurian Lodge of Druids'—a friendly society. By 1835, the **Mitre** was the base for 'The New Coach' which 'The Public are respectfully informed ... has commenced running, and will continue to leave the above Hotel every Tuesday, Thursday and Saturday, passing through Ross, Coleford, Saint Briavels, Chepstow, Bristol and will arrive at the White Lion, Bath at 4 o'clock.'

By 1892, the proprietresses, Misses A. & M. Williams, were proud to say: 'Of course, there are degrees of comfort to be obtained even in Hotels, and at the **Mitre**, at Hereford, the maximum seems to have been reached.' By this time the new tourist was an important customer: 'The Misses Williams ... like nothing better than to offer a hearty welcome to the constant bands of touring cyclists, who make it their temporary abiding place. The Cycling Tourists' Club have, in fact, appointed it headquarters for their numberless members. No mean recommendation, for it recognises that here good accommodation is combined with a reasonable tariff.' This was many years before the Youth Hostels Association was founded.

In the early 20th century the fascia board read '**Mitre Hotel**, Stables and Garage' and there was, and still is, a wide driving-way leading into the rear yard. The main entrance still boasts its wrought iron portico, cast at the short-lived Hereford Foundry in Friar Street, which, when the building was still an inn, was used regularly as a platform for parliamentary figures to address their supporters.

The remaining twelve years of the lease on the **Mitre** was sold in 1943 for £13,000. At this time the public entry was through revolving doors into the lounge and saloon bar, whilst across the yard was the Mitre Vaults containing public and private bars. There had been some trouble with the Vaults in 1913, presumably because of their out-of-the-way situation in the yard. It was resolved when the manager of the **Mitre** agreed that if a summons was withdrawn then he would close the Vaults for the sale of beer and only use them for wines and spirits. He also agreed to remove the seating accommodation, the bar and the smoking room. Presumably the intention was to restrict the use to people who just wanted a quick drink—hence the removal of the seating. Such spartan conditions would hardly appeal to the residents! At that time there were 13 double and 5 single letting bedrooms, mainly fitted with washbasins, but only two bathrooms are mentioned. The lease came to an end and the **Mitre** finally closed to customers on the 28th September, 1955, to become yet another bank to add to the growing number in Broad Street.

The eastern side of Broad Street had at least one more inn during the 19th century. This was the **Globe Tavern** which was one of the range of buildings that then faced King Street and backed onto the Cathedral Close. The **Globe** was a popular pub sign throughout the country and apart from its obvious world-wide associations could also be linked with the Shakespearian Globe Theatre.

In 1839, the landlord of the Hereford **Globe**, one Benjamin Mills, advised 'his Friends and the Public generally ... that his reading room will be opened and that a person will attend each evening as public reader to the company.' The papers taken in were a London Daily, the *Weekly Dispatch*, the *Hereford Times* and the *Hereford Journal*. Inns are no longer purveyors of news—the 'public readers' who are now employed by the broadcasting authorities are doubtless much better paid than their earlier counterparts who had to find employment in the city taverns!

By 1842, Mr. Mills was able to advertise a reduction in the price of his home-brewed ale to four pence per quart. During the same year he held a dance on the premises to celebrate the christening of the Prince of Wales, eldest son of Queen Victoria and later to become Edward VII. Notwithstanding all Benjamin Mills' efforts, the **Globe** closed its doors some time around the 1860's and was then converted to an apartment house—a use which continued for many years. However, a fire in the adjoining building, which occurred on the 29th April 1935, was the final blow and less than a month later the whole block of buildings was demolished, exposing the cathedral to the view of pedestrians in Broad Street for the first time.

One inn, which in 1739 was described as being in Broad Street near to the cathedral, has not been accurately positioned. An early advertisement reads:

'A cock match to be fought at Mr. Joseph Grice's at the **Ship and Castle** in Hereford between the gentlemen of Staffordshire and the gentlemen of Monmouthshire: to shew 41 cocks on a side in a main, for 10 guineas a battle and 200 guineas the odd battle, and 10 cocks on a side for Bye-Battles, for 4 guineas a battle. To weigh on Monday, the 7th day of May next, and to fight the three following days'.

The high stakes operating at this match and at others held in the city in the 18th century demonstrate the popularity of this 'sport' amongst the upper classes throughout the region.

Towards the end of the 19th century the west side of Broad Street had a wide variety of Hotels, Inns and Taverns, but all have now closed apart from the **Green Dragon** which has grown from relatively humble beginnings to become the premier hotel in the city.

Facing the **City Arms**, and on the opposing corner to the **Queen's Arms**, was the appropriately named **King's Head**. This was probably the hostelry that was then called the **King's Inn** and described as being 'in the North Gate', which offered good accommodation for guests and provided saddle horses to let in 1792. Even then it was well-established, for the accounts of the Mercers Guild indicate that the **King's Head** was one of the principal inns of Hereford a century before that date. There was even a mention of a **King's Head** in 1639. Most of the inn signs with this name depict Henry VIII. This may well have been the case here, although the name could refer to Charles I, but only if his head was still on his shoulders for it was not until 1649 that he was beheaded!

Coaches ran from the **King's Head** to Aberystwyth during the first half of the 19th century. The landlord would open his house at five o'clock in the morning to serve 'early purl' to the travellers, and the coach would start on its mountainous journey at six. 'Purl' was originally made by infusing wormwood or other bitter herbs into ale or beer. As an early morning pick-me-up and a traveller's

The King's Head, built around 1900 and demolished in 1968

'tonic' it consisted of half a pint of boiled ale, a joey (two penny-worth) of gin, a little sugar and a pinch of ginger and was commonly known as a 'dog's nose'.

The **King's Head** was taken over by the Hereford Brewery probably when it was put up for sale in 1882. The sale details indicate that it was an important house with eight bedrooms, whilst the outline plan of the ground floor shows a site packed with buildings. A contemporary sketch looking from the courtyard gives a fair impression of the considerable age of the house. In 1898, when the Hereford Brewery and its hotels, public and beer houses were put up for sale, the **King's Head** had an annual value of £120—half as much again as the **Imperial Inn** and twice that of the **Grapes Tavern**. It was then described as having two public bars and a smoke room on the ground floor, but still had sufficient room for the Central Order Office for the Brewery.

The inn was then taken over by Samuel Allsopp & Co. and they employed the Hereford architectural firm of E.J. Bettington & Son to provide plans for a new building. The design, a slightly flam-boyant, three-storey, corner building, was typical of its period, and it was probably at that time that all traces of the historic coaching inn were lost forever.

The landlord fell foul of the law, as had happened at the **Garrick** in St. Peter's Street a month earlier. He was fined £4 in 1917 for serving after 9 p.m. Fortunately for him, the Hereford and Tredegar Brewery, who then owned the inn, took a more relaxed attitude to the official letter from Mr. Scobie, the Clerk to the Justices, and just acknowledged it without any comment whatsoever.

The rather splendid late-Victorian building, with its attached corner tower and dome, was in turn demolished in 1968, to be replaced with a prefabricated concrete and glass monstrosity with prominent bay windows that was immediately dubbed 'the Goldfish Bowl'. The new-look **King's Head** struggled on for a few years, but having neither atmosphere nor character it was unsuccessful in attracting customers. It was eventually sold and was then converted to offices for a building society.

Across West Street from the **King's Head** was the **Nag's Head**. The name probably refers to the availability of riding horses for hire at the inn rather than the presence of a shrewish woman! The **Nag's Head** is the fifth of the inns which once graced this cross roads (counting the **Punch Bowl** as well as the **Queen's**) and was of some size for it stretched back as far as Aubrey Street. The Whitefoot family were landlords during the 18th century, but it was not until the beginning of the 19th century that it became especially well-known for its fives court which filled the whole of the rear yard. It was also at the **Nag's Head** that the Nelson Society, which had been formed in 1805, met annually on October 21st, the anniversary of the Battle of Trafalgar.

In the 18th and early 19th centuries West Street was much narrower than it is today, and in 1865 it was decided that the **Nag's Head** should be demolished to allow the adjoining part of West Street to be widened to 18 feet. The reduced site was then rebuilt with a corner building and several shops facing on to West Street. The corner building was eventually used as a branch of the United Counties Bank. This was followed by Barclays Bank which was there for many years until it crossed the road after the closure of the **City Arms Hotel**.

Inns came thick and fast down Broad Street and next door to the **Nag's Head** was the **White Hart**. The **White Hart** was the heraldic symbol of Richard II and displaying it may have demonstrated the landlord's allegiance to Richard, although not to his usurper, Henry IV. This house also continued through to Aubrey Street, where there was a driving-way access. However, the Broad Street frontage was different to most Hereford inns for the access to the public house was through a narrow passage with shops on each side.

In 1746, the **White Hart** was described as an old and well-accustomed inn. Tea trading was carried out on the premises—it was still an expensive commodity, from eight shillings a pound for green tea to ten shillings for fine. Ten years later, the Masters of the Trade of Cordwainers (shoemakers) met at the house to discuss ways of suppressing unqualified persons.

By 1891 it was being described as the **White Hart Wine Vaults** and belonged to Arnold, Perrett & Co. who also used one of the shops as their office. The licence for the wine vaults was eventually surrendered in March 1937, as part of the deal to open the **Broad Leys** in Ross Road, although the brewery office continued to be used for some time.

But although the **White Hart** has long since closed, the building remains, and is of some considerable interest. Hidden behind the facade, which is merely an extension of that belonging to the **Green Dragon**, is a fine, early 17th century timber-framed house with equally early decorative plaster ceilings including vine, pomegranate, and fleur-de-lis. These excellent ceilings are in what was the sitting room on the first floor and in the bedroom above.

Formerly called the **White Lion**, the **Green Dragon** is now the largest hotel in Hereford. Its early history is largely unknown although there are several stories associated with it. It is difficult to credit the statement published early this century which suggested that it was used by people working on the reconstruction of the Cathedral in 1079 after its destruction by the Welsh. As a later writer suggests, 'there may be more truth in the story that the Earl of March (afterwards Edward IV) stayed there with his followers after the battle of Mortimer's Cross, and that Owen Tudor, who was defeated in that encounter, was confined there until his execution.' The earlier name may thus have some significance for the White Lion is the heraldic symbol for the Earls of March. The battle of Mortimer's Cross was in 1461 and following the battle, Owen Tudor, the grandfather of Henry VII, was beheaded in Hereford. According to one description his head was then washed, his hair and beard combed by 'a madwoman' and this grisly relic was then placed on top of the market cross surrounded by over a hundred candles.

Be that as it may, it is apparent that the **Green Dragon,** under whatever name, started its life as a small inn, no larger than others in the street. A green dragon is included in the arms of the Earls of Pembroke, who owned Goodrich Castle. It may be from such a source, rather than the usual 'George and Dragon' story that the inn got its name. It rapidly improved under the capable hands of the Bosely family; father John being landlord in 1831, followed by his sons, William and John, who eventually took over and ran both the **Green Dragon** and the **City Arms**. In the 1830's there was a coaching office at the **Green Dragon** and the Champion coach left there daily on its way to London. Trade was good, and in 1843 the Boselys' bought the adjoining properties. A few years later, in 1857, they erected the Italianate front which still survives. At the rear they built a large Assembly Room and by then could consider themselves as having the principal hotel in the city. It is not surprising that John became a Member of the City Council and was eventually elected Mayor in 1865.

The earliest friendly society in the city was established in 1766 at the **Bowling Green Inn**. It was called simply The Friendly Society

The Green Dragon showing the entrance to the driving-way

and by 1838, when its Articles were printed, it was meeting at the **Green Dragon**. Since its inception it had invested some £1,370 which had been collected from the members. Meetings were every third Thursday, the subscription 9d. The fee for dinner was two shillings with 3d. for the waiter from all, if present or not. There were rules against drunkenness, gaming and talking politics with a fine of half-a-crown or expulsion. By 1863 there were 81 members. The Society paid out sick pay, after five years membership, of thirty shillings weekly for sixteen weeks and twenty shillings thereafter. During the late 18th and 19th centuries there were many friendly societies of this nature in Hereford, mostly based on the inns and taverns.

Like many of the other hotels in the street, the **Green Dragon** continued through to Aubrey Street, but, reflecting its importance, coaches could arrive at the front and drive straight through the building. The driving-way was where the main entrance is now; the original front doorway being central to the triangular podium. The inn was enlarged in the early 1880's and again in 1913, when forty bedrooms were added.

The hotel had to follow the restrictive opening hours which had taken force during the First World War, and in 1920 the licensee successfully applied for a Market Licence, which allowed him to remain open between two-thirty and four on Wednesdays only.

On the 1st September, 1928, the **Green Dragon** took a full page advertisement in the *Hereford Times*. Describing itself as the 'Premier Hotel of the Wye Valley', the occasion was the completion of its new dining room, servery, kitchens, sculleries, still room, pantry and other facilities at a cost of some £12,000. The new dining room 'with comfortable seating for about 160 persons, is on the ground floor, with many large windows looking onto Broad Street. ... It has been panelled to the ceiling with British Oak, the design for which is adapted from a sixteenth century panelled room exhibited in the South Kensington Museum, and the wood was partly obtained from an immense oak felled on the Ox Pasture Farm in the parish of Marden in 1922 ... It is lighted, not only by the large windows on the street, but by an immense stone-mullioned and transomed window at the rear, which is filled with leaded lights'. It is not surprising that the proud management described it as 'the finest dining-room between Birmingham and Bristol'.

By 1930, the **Green Dragon** was ready to expand again and the two properties to the north were purchased for this purpose. During the demolition, a 14th century fireplace head and an early 17th century plaster ceiling were exposed and both were preserved within the new building. Although part of the extension incorporates a shop at ground-floor level, the classical facade of the Bosely brothers was continued across the new additions without any apparent break.

The large garage area, on the opposite side of Aubrey Street, which was eventually added to the Dragon empire, is not really part of this story, but it did allow the inn yard to be roofed over and the Broad Street driving-way to be totally removed.

Nowadays, the **Green Dragon** provides a degree of elegance to the central part of Broad Street, an elegance which is sadly lacking further south where the glass and concrete 1960's buildings are a poor substitute to the variety of buildings that previously graced this part of the street. In the middle of the 19th century the picture was totally different, for the street contained a whole series of inns stretching down as far as the Corn Exchange (later the Kemble Theatre).

Next door to the **Green Dragon**, after it had been extended, was the **Half Moon**, magnificently displayed with all its customers on a photograph which must be earlier than 1866 for that was the year that it was demolished and replaced by the stone-built County Club. It has been suggested that the name was derived from the semi-circular watch-towers on the city wall which were usually called

'half-moons'. The earliest mention of the inn was in 1775 when 'All that well accustomed inn the **Half Moon** in Broad Street with the stabling, yard and garden, let on a lease to Mr. Edward Davis at the yearly rental of £17 1s.' was for sale. At the rear was yet another fives court and the inn was once again the home to a flourishing friendly society.

The **Half Moon** was a double-frontage building being number 42 Broad Street. Next door, at number 41, was a small inn called the **Cross Keys**. Crossed keys are included in the papal arms, and the sign refers to St. Peter who held the keys to the kingdom of heaven. The inn is shown on Curley's 1858 plan, but had closed well before the end of the century. Next door again, which must have been number 40, was an inn which apparently kept changing its name. Around 1850 it was the **Prince of Wales** with J. Biddle as mine host. This would probably have referred to Edward (1841-1910), the eldest son of Queen Victoria, who was Prince of Wales for nearly 60 years before he became Edward VII in 1901. The inn name continued into the 1860's, but so famous was the landlord that it became known as **Biddle's House**. A new name was obviously needed when a change of landlord occurred and it first became the more prosaic **Exchange Refreshment Rooms** and then the **Exchange Hotel**. This lasted for quite a while until the inn was finally closed in December, 1927. The building was then converted into a now long-lost branch of a firm which is still well-known in Hereford—John Wilson, Ltd., Seedsmen.

There was one more building between **Biddle's House** and the Corn Exchange—this was number 39 and, not surprisingly, it was yet another inn called the **Garrick Hotel** or **Garrick Head**. This was one of several inns in the city which attempted to capitalise by using the name of Hereford's famous actor. It was functioning as a hotel in the middle of the 19th century and may have become the **Railway Inn**—a short-lived public house of the latter part of that century. It had been replaced with the premises of a hop and wool merchant well before 1891. During the 1930's the building became the Corporation Hop Warehouse.

CHAPTER FIVE

THE OLD TOWN:
WEST AND TOWARDS THE BRIDGE

Just as Broad Street was the main north-south road of the Saxon City, King Street and its continuation to the west, St. Nicholas Street, was the western part of the main west—east street which, it is assumed, continued through the northern part of Cathedral Close to join into Castle Street.

On the western side of Broad Street and parallel to it are Aubrey Street, originally called Wrothale—the street where the pig market was held—and Berrington Street, earlier called Plow Lane. Both run northwards from King Street as far as West Street, the road which ran just inside the northern defences of the Saxon town. The next street further west and still parallel to the others is Victoria Street. This was the road which originally ran outside the city ditch. After the defences fell into disuse, the ditch was gradually filled in and buildings were erected on top of the fill. This process was reversed in the mid-1960's when the Inner Relief Road was built by widening Victoria Street over the line of the old ditch and exposing a substantial length of the City Wall in the process.

King Street and St. Nicholas Street join at the top of Bridge Street, the road which leads down to the Old Wye Bridge. The junction is curiously wide, with the buildings on the north side set back in a slight arc. This open space was, until 1842, almost totally filled with the church of St. Nicholas. In one of the earlier attempts to resolve traffic problems in Hereford, this historic church was demolished and replaced with a new one a little distance to the west and just outside the city defences.

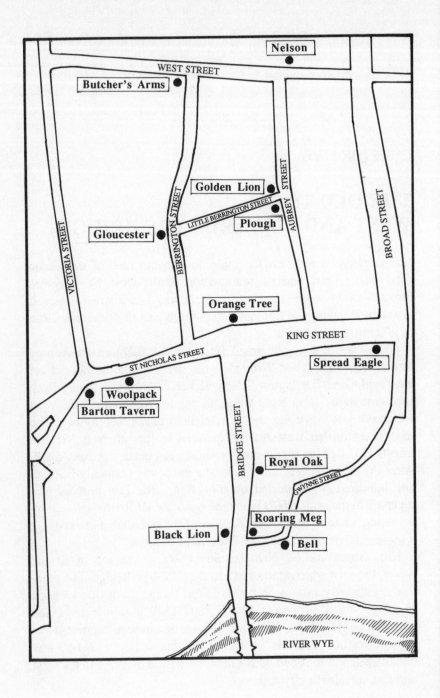

The city gate that stood at the junction of St. Nicholas Street and Victoria Street would have been the main gateway leading into the town during the Saxon period, but it became a minor gate after the city was extended to the north and a new west gate was built leading directly into the High Town market area. This minor gate, called Friars' Gate because there was a house of the Greyfriars a little distance outside and close to the river, was demolished by order of the Corporation in 1782. Between that date and 1798 all the city gates were demolished. Price, writing in 1796, expressed some reservations, commenting that 'the venerable aspect of the place [was] being injured, without an adequate acquisition of elegance.' The official policy was still included in a Directory half-a-century later: 'Their removal may be regretted by the antiquarian; but the superior healthiness of the city, now that no obstacle is offered to the free sweep of the winds, must be deemed an ample compensation.'

Bridge Street, leading down to the bridge across the River Wye, would have replaced the southern extension to Broad Street which originally led to the ford across the river. A connecting link, Gwynne Street, originally known as Pipe Lane or Pipewell Street, winds down from close to the entry to the Bishop's palace to join into Bridge Street close to the bridge. The date of the earliest bridge is uncertain, although it has been suggested that it was built around 800 A.D. The present bridge dates back at least as far as 1490, although it was widened in 1828. It continued to take all the traffic travelling up and down the main A49 Welsh border road until the new Greyfriars Bridge was built a little upstream in 1967.

Surprisingly, Bridge Street never seems to have had many inns. There was the **Boot**, which was sold on the 16th July 1784, but is otherwise unknown. One inn which closed many years ago was the **Old Pied Bull** which was on the corner of Gwynne Street and Bridge Street. When the owner, Herbert Rogers, died in 1718 he gave the yearly sum of £2, payable from the income of the house, to the poor of the parish of St. Nicholas. By the early 19th century it had suffered a name change to become the **Roaring Meg** after the historic cannon which had been used to batter down the walls of Goodrich Castle in 1646, towards the end of the Civil War. Colonel Birch had had it cast specially—presumably in a local forge—it was capable of throwing a two-hundredweight shell. His secretary, Roe, spoke of it with admiration 'by reason of a great mortarpiece you made there (the biggest in England) the enimy was terified, much of the inner part of the Castle ffalen downe, and the roofe spoyled.' Birch, being Governor of Hereford, brought Roaring Meg to the city and for many years it stood upside down as a corner-post at the corner of Gwynne Street and Bridge Street and outside the inn to which it gave its name. It was moved to Castle Green in 1839 and is now in the grounds of the Churchill Gardens Museum on Aylestone Hill. By 1861 the inn had become one of the several to be called the **St. Catherine Wheel** to be found in Hereford, but it must have closed shortly afterwards.

The **Royal Oak** was described in 1813 as being over 100 years old. This would have been named after the Boscobel Oak in which Charles II hid after his defeat at the Battle of Worcester in 1651. The inn was on the eastern side of Bridge Street, a couple of doors below the old Wesley Chapel—now a warehouse hidden behind a couple of shops—and is presently a night club called the Crystal Rooms. Nicholas Johnson, who retired as landlord in 1839, obviously enjoyed his stay there for he wrote that 'In retiring from this old-established Inn, [he] tenders his warmest wishes to the Agriculturalists of the County, Commercial Men, and the Public generally, for the flattering reception he met with upon his introduction into the City of Hereford, as well as for their continued patronage and support.' His son-in-law, James Lloyd, took over and apparently held regular Sweeps, for in 1842, amongst others, he advertised:

> The Cesarewith Stakes
> Newmarket, Oct. 1842
> 107 Subscribers at 5/- each
> 1st Prize £20
> 2nd Prize £6.15s.

To be drawn on Monday October 3rd at the **Royal Oak** Inn

He must have been depending on the sale of drink for his profit, for the whole of the subscription money went towards the two prizes!

The **Royal Oak** fronted onto Bridge Street whilst behind it, and approached by a narrow passage, was the Alhambra Theatre. This had been built as an annex to the inn in the 1830's. Made of wood, lit by gas and with poor ventilation, it was doubtless a considerable fire risk and highly dangerous. Even so, the theatre survived the inn by a few years, to be eventually closed in 1892. The Alhambra continued to be used as a seed store behind Franklin Barnes Shop (itself the old inn) until it was demolished in 1936.

On the opposite side of the street, the only inn that is still in operation in Bridge Street is the **Black Lion**. Although the black lion in many parts of the country refers to Phillipa, the wife of Edward III, the one in Hereford is more likely to be associated with Owain Glyndwr, who had a black lion in his arms. This is one of the oldest inns in Hereford to survive to the present day, but it has suffered many alterations since it was built. The main part of the building must date from the middle or second half of the sixteenth century, for it is to that period that the series of wall-paintings, found in the middle room on the first floor in 1932, are dated.

The **Black Lion** had been in use as an inn for many years when, in July 1778, there was the advertisement 'To be sold. A messuage or tenement known by the sign of the **Black Lion**, being a well-accustomed Inn situate in Wyebridge Street, in the occupation of Thomas Drew, with the garden, stables and Brewhouse'. The grounds were relatively long and narrow and stretched back as far as the City Wall, which formed the western boundary. The various outhouses associated with the inn were, and still are, in a long row against the northern boundary. The southern boundary of the plot was also the parish boundary separating St. Nicholas parish to the north from St. John's parish to the south.

Very late in the 19th century or early in the following one, the narrow property to the south of the parish boundary was added to the **Black Lion** establishment. Before that time, the entrance to the inn yard had been through the left-hand part of the original building, where there was a narrow driving-way. Radical alterations took place in 1910 when the southern property was completely demolished to provide a new and wider access to the yard. The old driving-way was then blocked up and converted to become the public bar. At that time the historic timberwork on the front elevation was exposed to view for a short period, but was not considered attractive at that time and was once again covered with render. The outhouses at the rear were converted into a games room and a new skittle alley, the latter replacing one which had been on stilts in the courtyard. Much of the rear yard then became a garage area covered with a corrugated iron roof.

The middle room on the first floor of the inn was then in use as a club room or dining room and was approached by a narrow stair from a rear lobby. At that time the wall-paintings had not been discovered, although the excellent arcaded overmantle and decorated plaster ceiling had been noted by the Royal Commission on Historic Monuments when they visited the inn in 1926. Their investigator came back again in 1932 following the exposure of the wall paintings. Fortunately, the Directors of the Stroud Brewery, to whom the house belonged, took a great interest in the discovery and commissioned Edward Long of Oxford to conserve the paintings.

'Thou shalt doo noe Murder'

The wall-paintings consist of a series of representations of people breaking the Ten Commandments. The first three had been destroyed long ago, and the series now begins with the 4th commandment—'Remember that thou keep holy the Sabbath day'—showing a man gathering sticks. The remaining six Commandments follow in series. Were these paintings made for the benefit of the landlord or his customers? We shall never be certain, but it is interesting to note that, following the Restoration in 1660, the various members of the Cathedral's historic Vicars' Choral began to join in the social life of the city and had 'frequent carousels at the **Black Lion** Club Room' as well as holding card parties in the **Coffee House** in Milk Lane, now St. John Street.

In the period between the two world wars, the house was always known as the **Black Lion Agricultural Inn** and had a rather forbidding exterior that had been rendered and lined to look like stone. The inn sign was just the simple name with, perhaps slightly more encouragingly underneath it 'Excellent garage for charsabanc, motors etc.' Neglecting the rather unusual spelling for charabanc, the present **Black Lion** has succeeded in gaining a much more friendly appearance since the render was removed, once again exposing the timber framework which is such a feature of this historic inn.

Wye Bridge House, the building nearest to the bridge on the upstream side, was a private hotel for much of the first half of the 20th century, but as such does not really come within the scope of this book. However, hidden behind the render is a fine timber-framed building which was included in the eighteen Hereford inns which were listed as historic buildings shortly after the 1947 Town and Country Planning Act was passed. The earliest documentary reference to the building is in 1586 when it was part of the Bodenham estate. In 1664, when Thomas and Sybil Lane lived there, it was assessed in the Hearth Tax for five hearths. The following year there had been an increase to nine hearths—a remarkably high number for all but the largest of private dwellings and one that suggests that it may well have been used as an inn. Sybil Lane died in 1678 and the inventory following her death shows that she was brewing on the premises, reinforcing this suggestion.

The passage entry to Gwynne Street is almost opposite the **Black Lion**. It was so named because Nell Gwynne, the mistress of Charles II, was reputedly born there in 1650. Although very much a back lane, it was the home for the **Starre**, mentioned in 1623. Was this named after the sixteen-pointed star in the arms of the Worshipful Company of Innholders or was it the pole star, one of the seven stars which make up the constellation Ursa Major? If it was the latter then this could well be the same establishment where, almost two hundred years later there was advertised: 'At the sign of the **Seven Stars** in Pipe Lane in this city on Monday June 27th, 1808. To be sold: A complete and well built Barge called the Valiant, 32 tons'.

Barges had been using the River Wye for the transport of heavy goods, and particularly coal from the Forest of Dean, on a regular basis since the early 18th century. The return journeys downstream took the county products, including oak bark (for tanning), cider, corn, and wood. Barges were built locally on the river banks; they were pulled upstream by teams of five or six men except for the odd occasions when sails could be used.

The **Starre** and the **Seven Stars** were both in Gwynne Street and are apparently earlier names for a more well-known inn, the **Bell**, which is first mentioned the year after the last reference to stars, single or multiple in Gwynne Street. The **Bell** is shown on the 1858 map of the city as being on the river side of the lane, by the first bend and just before the entrance to the grounds of Gwynne House. In the 1830's it was run by Charles James, who also dealt in the wholesale wine and spirit trade. In the inn he sold 'Porter in bottle and cask, prime bottled cider and perry, the Pale Indian ale, and strong beer 3 and 4 years old, in addition wines, spirits and pure malt liquors'. He advertised well-aired beds and was able to produce 'chops, steaks etc on the shortest notice'.

The **Bell** was renowned for being the headquarters of the bargemen and, when it was put up for sale in 1842, it was described as:

'All that compact and substantially built freehold messuage, replete with every requisite convenience for carrying on an extensive business, together with the Brew House, excellent stables, spacious yard and other convenient warehouses, storehouses etc., behind the same, called or known by the name of the **Bell Inn**, situate in Pipe Lane, in the City of Hereford, in the occupation of Mr. Joseph Wood.'

The sale details described the inn as being 'old-established' and also explained that the yard had a communication with the River Wye and that the warehouses could, at a trifling expense, be converted into a malthouse. There was a wharf on the river bank in front of the **Bell** and the reason for the suggestion that the warehouses could be converted to an alternative use may well have been because of their lack of use by traffic on the Wye following the completion of the horse-drawn tramroad in 1829, which brought coal from South Wales, and the anticipated arrival of the Gloucester to Hereford canal, which was finally opened to Hereford in 1845.

The **Bell** struggled on for a few more years, but as the barge traffic on the Wye decreased, so did the trade at the inn. It was still functioning in 1858 with Mr. T. Easthope as landlord, but closed well before the end of the century.

In King Street is the **Spread Eagle Hotel**. The spread eagle was originally a Roman emblem and came into English heraldry after the Crusades. It has strong relationships with several European countries including Austria, Germany, Russia, Spain and France. Still with its driving-way, which originally led to the stables and later to the garage in the yard, this old-established inn dates back to the early 17th century. However the cellar is much earlier, for it is of late medieval date with stone walls and a central octagonal column complete with a moulded capital. Changes to the inn have been relatively minimal and the original separation into individual small rooms on the ground floor is still preserved. The front door still opens into what was the public bar and the side door leads into the lounge and the upstairs rooms. For many years the **Spread Eagle** belonged to the Alton Court Brewery Co. Ltd.; it is now a Whitbread house. Next door, at number 3, during the late 19th century, was the Palace Hotel, a 'commercial and private boarding house'.

Continuing along King Street, across the top of Bridge Street into St. Nicholas Street, and at the end of the terrace of houses, is a visible trace of a small Hereford inn that did not renew its licence at the Sessions as long ago as February 1905 and had become an apartment house by 1917. This was the **Woolpack** which was certainly in operation in the 1850's and quite possibly for some time earlier. The woolpack was a bale of wool which weighed some 240lb. and there are many inns with the same name in those areas where there was once a thriving wool trade. The building has a stone string course which separates the ground and first floor windows on the street facade and on this can still be seen painted **Woolpack, Wine & Spirit Vaults**. The large cellars with a barrel-roll within the stair entry and containing a well, may suggest that it was built for use as a small inn.

Across the road from the **Woolpack**, at the junction of St. Nicholas Street and King Street and facing down Bridge Street, is the **Orange Tree**. This is reputed to be one of the oldest pubs in the city originally called the **Apple Tree** before being transformed into a more exotic fruit. Orange trees were first imported into this country in the late 16th century by Sir Thomas Gresham founder of the Royal Exchange and a Merchant Adventurer. However, the present building, which is probably no earlier than the early 17th century, had substantial alterations in the 1840's when it was totally re-fronted in brick. It was about this time that the historic St.

Nicholas Church, which stood in the middle of the road directly in front of the inn, was demolished. Perhaps the opening up of the street, which followed this act of vandalism, was the catalyst for the landlord to carry out his own 'improvements' by removing the half-timbered facade and replacing it with plain brick.

By 1907, this rather plain appearance was not satisfactory for the owners, the Hereford and Tredegar Brewery Ltd., and it was once again re-faced, this time with bay windows at first-floor level and larger 'inn-style' windows on the ground floor. The first-floor level was roughcast and the ground floor was rendered in cement and lined to look like stone. Since then there has been no external alterations, but the interior has had several changes, the last in 1989. The main effect of this last improvement was to totally remove the long passage which went down the eastern side of the building so as to open up the ground floor and expose the early 17th century moulded panelling which graces the full length of the eastern wall.

The inn suffered like many others from the restrictions on opening times which were imposed during the First World War. These regulations continued to be stringently enforced, for in 1920, the landlord, John Richard Sharpe, was fined the relatively large sum of £10 for supplying intoxicating liquor to his own son and a friend during prohibited hours. His son and friend were also summoned for aiding and abetting and the former was fined £2 whilst his friend, Leonard Clarke, got away with £1.

Unfortunately, on the 14th of April 1994, the inn suffered from a fire which caused extensive damage to the roof and upper levels and much devastation internally from water. At the time of writing it presents a rather sorry appearance with a tarpaulin over the roof. Substantial repair work including a new extension at the rear are planned by the owners, Whitbreads.

There were several small public houses in the side streets to the north of King Street and St. Nicholas Street. This area of the city suffered from a lack of a firm planning policy both before and after the Second World War, when many buildings, including several of considerable historic interest, disappeared without trace. The timber-framed almshouses, which still survive in Berrington Street, give a slight impression of what this area must have been like.

One of the oldest inns in this area was the **Gloucester**, or **Gloucestershire House** as it was often called. The inn was one half of a 17th century timber-framed terrace of two houses on the western side of Berrington Street, almost opposite the narrow Little Berrington Street which joins Berrington Street to Aubrey Street. The garden behind the inn extended as far as the city wall and must at one time have provided a grand view westwards towards the Black Mountains. This house was called the **Last Inn** during the latter part of the 18th century when it was rented by Mr. T.K. Went in 1796 for £16 per year.

The Gloucester shortly after closure

In 1915, William Collins described the **Gloucester** in his *Historical Landmarks of Hereford* as 'This fine old half-timbered building belongs to the Stuart period, and has been recently restored at the cost of the trustees of St. Giles' Hospital (to whom it belonged). The old-fashioned signboard, suspended on chains from an oak beam, has been added through the generosity of Mr. John Lambe, solicitor, Bridge Street. For many years its heavy timbers have been covered with plaster; all this has been removed, and the building is seen in its original form and beauty, leaded lights being substituted for windows that were somewhat out of harmony with the surroundings.' Inside, the Royal Commission inspectors visiting in 1928 noted a staircase with twisted balusters; at that time the building was in good condition.

However, it had ceased to operate as an inn a few years earlier for this was one of the houses which were closed by the Licensing Committee in 1919. The Commission paid compensation of £450 to extinguish the licence of the **Gloucestershire House**, as they described it in their annual report and noted that they had, by then, extinguished 35 licences. In the Directories around the turn of the century, the occupier of the **Gloucester** is described as a 'beer retailer', for this establishment never had a wine and spirits licence, being merely a beer-house. It was eventually demolished in 1938 and replaced with nondescript warehousing.

Along Little Berrington Street to the junction with Aubrey Street and the turn of the century walker would have found two inns, one on each corner. On the northern side was the **Golden Lion** whilst opposite it was the **Plough**.

In the mid-19th century the **Golden Lion** was known as the **Cross Arrow**, and is shown as such on the 1858 plan. It survived until February 1954 when the licence was surrendered on the granting of the one for the **Belmont Inn** in Belmont Road. The landlord then moved to the **Whalebone** in Eign Road. The **Golden Lion** was a rather gaunt brick building, a full three stories high, the impression of height being increased by the three stone steps that led up to the front door. It was not long after closure that the building was demolished.

The **Plough** was a much older building, two stories high with a rough-cast render that probably concealed a timber frame. The sign

could refer to the seven stars which form the shape of a plough in the constellation of Ursa Major, or to the rather obvious agricultural implement. There were five well-worn stone steps up to the front door of the inn from Little Berrington Street. The **Plough** continued in use until the 19th February, 1937, when the license was surrendered to allow the **Game Cock** in Holme Lacy Road to open. The building was then taken over by Sid Wright Ltd., the fruit and vegetable wholesaler, who was rapidly expanding at that time. The firm had started in 1935 in Eign Street, but within five years had obtained property in West Street, and had expanded the business to Kington and Leominster. Next door to the **Plough** in the 1950's was Wright's Food Bazaar—perhaps the earliest supermarket in the city! The wholesale department was in the old inn—Sid Wright,

The Plough in Little Berrington Street

with some nostalgia, continued to advertise it as 'The Sign of the Plough'. Of course, the building was not really suitable for its new use, and it was eventually demolished to make way for a larger warehouse, which in turn has been demolished to provide yet more parking space for cars.

The **Butchers Arms** stood on the western corner of Berrington Street, a couple of doors up from what is now the Regal, but was earlier the Picture House, then the Palladium, and eventually the County Cinema. But all that was after the **Butchers Arms** had finally closed for, although it was in full operation in the mid-19th century, the licence was not renewed in 1897. At that time the Regal was the Beethoven Hall—the piano and parlour-organ show-room for George Heins—hardly a source of trade for the **Butchers Arms**! Perhaps, had the inn survived until the moving pictures arrived in 1913, it would still have been there today.

The **Nelson** in West Street, facing the end of Aubrey Street, almost followed the **Butchers Arms** into oblivion, for it was closed in January 1966 and remained empty for many years throughout the 1970's and early '80's before being rescued and renamed the

NELSON INN, HEREFORD.

HEREFORD, LEOMINSTER, AND LUDLOW

ACCOMMODATION.

THE Public are most respectfully informed, that a NEW COACH leaves the NELSON every Morning (except Sunday) at half-past Nine, arrives at the OAK INN, Leominster, at a quarter-past Eleven, and FEATHERS INN, Ludlow, at One. Leaves Ludlow at Three in the Afternoon, and arrives in Hereford at half-past Six.

The Public patronage is most respectfully solicited, as every attention will be paid to passengers.

Parcels delivered punctually by the sole Proprietor,
EDWARD SHEPLEY.

Stagecoach. Although now combining a restaurant and steak house, it still functions essentially as an inn. The **Nelson** was built early in the 17th century on top of the remains of the Saxon defensive rampart. At its rear there would originally have been a water-filled ditch, probably used as an open sewer, which would have prevented any direct access through to Eign Street. However, there must have been ample room for a courtyard and stables as the driving–way through the building still survives.

It doubtless had an earlier name, but was called the **Lord Nelson** almost immediately after the famous admiral came to Hereford in 1802 to be made a freeman of the city. When it was for sale in 1836 it was described as:

'All that substantial Freehold Messuage or dwelling house, now in full business called the **Nelson Inn**, most desirably situated in Packers Lane, at the top of the Sheep and Pig Markets, together with Brewhouse and other convenient offices, excellent arched Cellaring, a very substantial brick built Malthouse, and six messuages or tenements situate in Cooke's Square, adjoining to the said **Nelson** Inn.'

Cooke's Square may well have been the inn yard or the courtyard to the east, both of which could have contained several of the small one-up-one-down tenements which were typical of the backland areas of Hereford and many other towns in that period. By this time the prefix 'Lord' had been dropped from the name and it had become a local coaching inn. Coaches left daily at 9.30 a.m., taking an hour and three-quarters to get to Leominster and three-and-a-half hours to Ludlow. The trade must have been successful for by 1839, the new landlord, William Watkins, was advertising that 'the recent enlargements and improvements he has made render his House more commodious than it formerly was' and that it would be 'his constant study to merit their esteemed favours'. He also had warehouse rooms to let for hops and wool. A year later he was able to supply families with 'good home-brewed beer and, being his own Maltster, he is enabled to offer it in cask or otherwise at the most reasonable prices.' He provided travellers with 'well-aired beds' and, by 1842, he had a horse and phaeton to let.

Landlords seem to change quite regularly, even when they appear to be successful, and by 1847 Thomas Coffey held the **Nelson**. He was still there in 1858, but by 1876 Thomas Rudge had taken over, to be replaced by Samuel Pritchard and, up to the turn of the century, by Mrs. Sarah Skyrme—all good Herefordshire names, reflecting the typical landlord of the day. The building has had a rough-cast render on the West Street face for many years and has a brick extension on the east. However, the original timber framework is still visible on the western side. Here is evidence that the roof was heightened to the front at one time. Before this the head room at first-floor level must have been very restricted—was this the work of William Watkins in 1839, designed to make the inn 'more commodious'?

The **Nelson**, or **Stagecoach**, as we must call it now, includes some shops in the courtyard on the east and accommodation at the rear of the yard—not all that much different to 150 years ago when it was one of the most thriving inns of the city.

CHAPTER SIX

THE OLD TOWN: THE EASTERN SIDE

Broad Street, the main street of the Saxon city, continued to have an important status throughout the medieval period up to the present day. In essence, it split the old city into two parts—the western part, described in the previous chapter, and the eastern section, which includes Church Street, St. John Street, Ferrers Street and St. Ethelbert Street, all running parallel to Broad Street and joining East Street at the north to Cathedral Close and Castle Street, the eastern continuation of the line of King Street at the south.

It is immediately obvious that, apart from Church Street, this part of the city has for many years been mainly residential and as a result did not contain the inns and public houses that were common elsewhere. Much of this area was where the cathedral dignitaries had their houses in large grounds—some, such as 20 Church Street, Harley House, 5 St. John Street and Harley Court, still survive— and where Georgian houses were built by the entrepreneurs of the day. Not for them the common inn on the doorstep!

Church Street is split into two parts; the wider section from Cathedral Close up to East Street and the narrow passage which leads from there through into High Town. This passage, like others further to the east, was created over 900 years ago by the Saxon residents of the old town making efforts to gain access to the new Norman Market Place in High Town and St. Peter's Square. They had to scramble from the main part of Church Street up onto the top of the defensive embankment, drop down the face of the stone wall, and then cross the water-filled ditch, probably by a plank bridge.

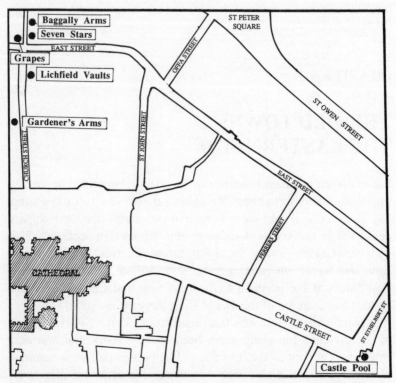

This, then, was the beginning of what was called in the 13th century Cabocheslone. In the 15th century the two parts were separately identified as Brode Cabeige Lane and Narowe Cabeige Lane, which was gentrified in the 18th century to Capuchin Lane. The 19th century saw it become Church Street with the narrow section being called, rather confusingly as it was furthest from the river, Lower Church Street.

This narrow passage was host to several small inns of which only the **Grapes Tavern** remains. On the opposite corner was the **Seven Stars** and three doors nearer High Town was the **Butchers Arms**. The butchers of Hereford must have been thirsty people for there was already a **Butchers Arms** in Berrington Street. The Butchers Company was granted arms in 1540. Little is known about the

Butchers Arms in Lower Church Street, which is shown on the 1858 map, but was apparently closed shortly afterwards as it is not included in the Directory for that year. However, there is a mention of the **Baggally Arms**, described as being in Lower Church Street in 1862 with Thomas Allsop Francis as landlord—could this have been a slightly later name for the **Butchers Arms**? Whatever its final name, the inn eventually closed, but the building still survives as number 5 Church Street. It was built early in the 19th century and has a fine, early 20th century shop-front containing large curved-glass bays and a central, recessed doorway.

The **Seven Stars** also survives, although it is now a restaurant. It had a longer life than the **Butchers Arms** for it was in existence in 1858 and continued in use into the early years of the present century, finally closing in 1913. It started its life in the early 19th century corner building, but must have been successful for it expanded into the garden area at the rear of the two adjoining houses in Lower Church Street, numbers 6 and 7. Here a two-storey extension had been built by the mid-19th century. The building has a curved corner incorporating the present doorway, with a large window to Church Street. The original entrance was on East Street and, though it has been bricked up for many years, curiously still retains its pediment. The section of the building to the rear has since been restored to numbers 6 and 7 Church Street which are now joined to form a single unit. Since the incorporation of number 2 East Street into that complex, it completely surrounds the old **Seven Stars**.

The **Grapes Tavern** is now a well-cared-for and attractive pub which makes a positive contribution to the streetscape of this part of the city. It forms an end piece to Upper Church Street and is one of the few remaining historic buildings on the north side of East Street. But it is only a few years ago that it was closed and boarded up with extensive external shoring and massive weighted scaffolding on the inside to prevent the front wall from collapsing into East Street.

Like several other buildings constructed within the narrow stretch of ground between St. Peter's Street, High Town, High Street and Eign Gate Street on the north and East Street and West Street on the south, the **Grapes** overlies the remains of the Saxon defences of the city. Once the High Town Market Place was constructed, the defences would have become redundant, and medieval buildings could well have been erected on the **Grapes** site. At this time West Street and East Street were known collectively as Byhindewallestrete reflecting their position relative to the disused defences, but by the 16th century they were becoming known as Packers Lane. It was the mid-19th century that produced the descriptive but boring West Street and East Street. The change between them was originally at Church Street, but is now at Broad Street. The confusion was well illustrated by the **Grapes** which was described as being next to 47 West Street in 1891, but had become 39 Church Street in 1935.

But the story of the inn goes back much further to when, in the early 19th century, it was called the **Royal Oak and Grapes**. This was about the time, shortly after the death of George IV, when its customers were certainly very active. It was in June, 1832, that the news that the Reform Bill had passed the House of Lords reached Hereford. This was the first of the five Reform Acts which were eventually to give everyone over the age of 21 the right to vote (the 1969 Act reduced the voting age from 21 to 18). The 1832 Reform Act did away with rotten boroughs and pocket boroughs and, generally speaking, gave the vote to the male members of the middle classes who had previously not had that privilege. Apparently the customers of the **Grapes** had sent a petition for the reform and, on hearing the news, they triumphantly raised a full length portrait of Earl Grey, the leader of the ruling Whig party, adorned with laurel. The Mayor arranged for the town to be decorated and there was a procession with a band and flags. There would seem to be no doubt that the worthy tradesmen who frequented the **Grapes** took a leading part.

In 1837 the **Grapes** was described as a tavern that had been run by Mrs. Almond and her late husband for 'a long period'. It was offered for sale by auction in that year, but may not have been sold, for in May 1839 it was again on the market. Failing to find a buyer by private contract it was once again put up for auction in September of that year when it was described as:

'All that extensive and old established Inn, in full trade, situate at the corner of Capuchin Lane and Packers Lane, and fronting Church Street, the greatest thoroughfare in the City, leading to the

Cathedral, now in the occupation of the proprietor, and known by the name of the **Grapes Tavern and Wine Vaults**. The House consists of a roomy and well appointed Bar, 3 large Parlours and Taproom, cooking Kitchen, back Kitchen, 2 Larders, a Pantry and Brewhouse, Furnaces etc., on the Ground Floor, also a large detached Dining Room and Premises capable of dining 60 persons; 4 good bedrooms, and sitting room, on the first floor; 3 bedrooms on the second; and a very excellent attic over the whole. The Cellarage is deep, dry, stone built, and extending nearly under the whole building; there is a paved yard attached, with stable and store room; the frontage is 90 feet, and depth 78; in good repair, being just completed, and fit for the most extensive business. There is a Pew in the Church of St. Peter's appurtenant to the House.'

The present frontage of 59 feet and depth of 53 feet demonstrate the losses which have occurred during the last 150 years. They included the covered passageway and one other building along East Street and probably the brewhouse and detached dining room at the rear, demolished many years ago and now lost within the Marks and Spencer store. It is apparent that in the middle of the 19th century the **Grapes** was one of the principal hostelries in the city.

Henry Butt bought the **Grapes** and immediately sold the stock-in-hand at reduced prices, meanwhile assuring his potential customers that the ale he was presently brewing would be 'of first-rate quality'. The following year he advertised:

Now's the time my boys
If you wish to taste the real old Nut Brown Ale
Call at the Grapes Tavern—Church Street
Where that most delicious beverage may now be had
in all its purity and perfection
AND NO MISTAKE

After some ten years at the **Grapes**, Henry Butt opened his 'Newly Established Gin and Brandy Vaults, having entered into arrangements with some of the first importers and rectifiers in the metropolis.' He stayed at the Tavern until the early 1870's and was followed for a short while by Thomas Cotten and then Henry Watkins.

It must have been during this period that the **Grapes** had an official reader of the news, appointed to read to the customers. Until

The reading room in the Grapes Tavern before restoration

the recent alterations, the room in which the news was read was virtually unaltered—it has now lost a little of the character by being opened through to the rear covered courtyard, but still retains much of the atmosphere. The room is fitted with wall seating where each seat has arm rests. The flavour is caught perfectly in a description published many years ago in the Transactions of the Woolhope Club:

'These chairs were occupied by men who were duly and solemnly elected to them, and here substantial tradesmen met every night to drink, smoke and gossip. When the occupant of a chair died, it was left empty until after his funeral. His mug, or tankard, was placed on the table in front of his chair. This was covered with black crepe, and his long churchwarden pipe laid across the top. After the funeral a new tenant was elected.'

The news of the fall of Sebastopol (in 1854) and of the Indian Mutiny (in 1857) were both read out in this room.

Until recently there was a plaque on the wall outside the **Grapes** which read, slightly inaccurately:

Ye Olde Bunch of Grapes
The original oak-panelled room with armed seating where the
London Letter
(which was delivered weekly by Stage Coach)
was read by a Chairman appointed annually to the office,
remains almost untouched.

The inn had belonged to the Whitbread group for many years before it was closed in 1988. When the full extent of the necessary repair work became obvious, they decided to put the building on the market. It was then that the City Council commissioned the City of Hereford Archaeology Unit to carry out a full survey and analysis. The survey was detailed—each timber frame was drawn with every individual timber, mortice, tenon and peg-hole carefully marked in place. The analysis which followed demonstrated that the **Grapes** consisted of three separate buildings, two of 17th century date and one of the late 18th century. All three had suffered from many alterations and repairs, some of which had been detrimental to the fabric and had helped to create the problems which the architect had to resolve. The earliest part of the building includes some of the walls in the cellars which are made of well-squared stone. They probably belonged to an otherwise unknown building, demolished in the 17th century to make way for the present structure.

There is now only one inn between East Street and the Cathedral Close, namely the **Lichfield Vaults** on the eastern side of Church Street. At an earlier date it was called the **Dog Inn**, and as such was mentioned in 1782 and 1799, and again as late as 1872. However, neither the **Dog** nor the **Lichfield Vaults** are shown on the 1858 city map or in the Directory for that year. Whatever was happening at that time, the name change had occurred by 1900, probably due to a change of ownership, for in 1914, when alterations were proposed, the proprietors were given as 'The Lichfield Brewery Co. Ltd.' Before the alterations, the ground floor plan consisted of a large L-shaped smoke room with wall seating and two fireplaces towards the rear of the building and approached by a long side passage. At the front was a minute bar, about 8 feet long by 5 feet wide—smaller than a prison cell—and inevitably with standing room only. There was a double gable on the front which had been rendered, but could well have been timber-framed underneath.

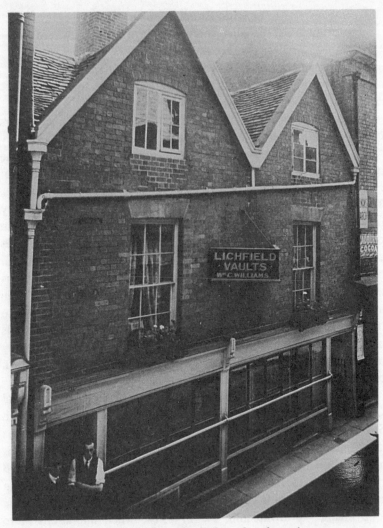

The Lichfield Vaults before the alteration

The proposals were radical for that time as they envisaged one large room containing both bar and smoke room. But such a scheme may well have alienated the customers from both sides as a handwritten note was added to the plans to provide a screen between the two parts. The proprieties were preserved and the separation between workmen and tradesmen was to continue for another half-century.

There is little to be said about other inns which once plied their trade in Church Street. **The Gardeners Arms** was on the opposite side to the **Lichfield Vaults**, but nearer to the cathedral. It was operating in 1872 and survived for some forty years or so, closing a couple of years after the beginning of the 20th century. One inn has only a single mention—this was the **Carpenters Arms**, described as being for sale in 1867—was this an earlier and even less successful name for the inn which then became the **Gardeners**?

One of the places frequented by the Vicars' Choral in the 17th century and later was the **Coffee House** in Milk Lane. It was not unusual at that time to dignify a common ale-house by calling it a Coffee House—an inn in everyhting but name! Milk Lane was an early name for St. John Street which joins East Street to the north-eastern corner of Cathedral Close. In 1826, Edward Wilding at the Sign of the **Coffee House** paid the sum of thirty pounds as Alehouse Keeper's Recognizance, as a surety of his good behaviour. He agreed to:

'Keep the true Assize in uttering and selling Bread and other Victuals, Beer, Ale, Cider, and other Liquors, in his House, and shall not fraudulently dilute or adulterate the same, and shall not use, in uttering and selling there-of, any Pots or other Measures that are not of full size, and shall not wilfully or knowingly permit Drunkenness or Tippling, nor get drunk in his House, or other Premises; nor knowingly suffer any Gaming with Cards, Draughts, Dice, Bagatelle, or any other sedentary Game in his House, or any of the Outhouses, Appertenances, or Easements thereto belonging, by Journeymen, Labourers, Servants, or Apprentices; nor knowingly introduce, permit, or suffer any Bull, Bear, or Badger-baiting, Cock-fighting, or other such Sport or Amusement, in any part of his Premises; nor shall knowingly or designedly and with a view to harbour and entertain such, permit or suffer Men or Women of notoriously bad fame, or dissolute Girls and Boys, to assemble and meet together, in his House, or any of the Premises thereto belonging; nor shall keep open his House, nor permit or suffer any Drinking or Tippling in any part of his Premises, during the usual Hours of Divine Service on Sundays; nor shall keep open his House or other Premises during late Hours of the Night or early in the Morning, for any other purpose than the Reception of Travellers, but do keep good Rule and Order therein, according to the purport of a License granted for Selling Ale, Beer, or other Liquors, by Retail, in the said House and Premises, for One whole Year commencing on the Tenth day of October next.'

This Recognizance gives a vivid impression of events which had previously taken place in the public houses of Hereford, but which had been banned by the early nineteenth century. The **Coffee House** in Milk Lane was closed before the middle of the century.

One hotel within this part of the old town is relatively new as a licensed premises. This is the **Castle Pool Hotel** which seals the eastern end of Castle Street and has large gardens overlooking the Castle Pool, once part of the moat which surrounded Hereford Castle. The main part of the castle is now open parkland stretching between the Castle Pool and the River Wye. There is little trace of the castle that Leland described in the mid-sixteenth century as being 'of as great circuite as Windesore and which had been one of the fairest, largest and strongest castles of England'. The main entrance to the castle was on the north side, across the Castle Pool at the end of the Hotel garden. There Leland saw 'a great bridge of stone archis, and a draw bridge in the midle of it, to entre into the castle. It is now clene downe'.

The **Castle Pool Hotel** was built as a pair of late Georgian houses but was altered to become a single residence with a two-bay pediment on giant pilasters. As Castle Pool House, it was the home of Frederick Joseph Boulton around the turn of the century. By 1929, it had become the **Castle Pool Hotel** with Mrs. Diver and Miss Beasley as proprietresses. It started as a private hotel but, by 1941, it was included in the Directories along with the other principal hotels of the county. Mrs. Diver must have enjoyed her work, for she stayed for many years and was still listed as the proprietress in 1950. However, it did not obtain a 'restaurant and residential licence' until July, 1967.

CHAPTER SEVEN

INSIDE THE CITY WALLS:
THE NORTH-WESTERN CORNER

When William fitzOsbern built his new Market Place to the north
of the Saxon town, he also created a series of wide approach roads,
appropriate to the status of his new town. They all led into the
market place and were streets in which his new French settlers
could build their houses.

For Welshmen arriving from the west there was the imposing
Eign Street, known as Guldefordstrete in the 13th century. This was
not the narrow Eign Gate Street we know now; the original street
was wide enough to include Bewell Street as well. The row of
buildings which now runs between the two, stretching as far as All
Saints Church, is the final result of market stalls gradually
becoming more permanent until they actually included living
accommodation as well.

Visitors from the south and east—the Gloucester and Ledbury
directions—would have entered along St. Owen Street, the
Hungreystrete of the middle ages, still a wide street all the way to
St. Peter's Square and church, the beginning of the market place.

Arriving from Bromyard or Worcester, the traveller had the
height of Aylestone Hill to conquer before he saw Hereford in front
of him. The road was a wide sweep, all the way down the hill to a
bridge crossing of the Widemarsh or Eign brook after which it
widened again to form the present Commercial Road, earlier known
as Bye Street, which led directly into the market.

One main road was part of the Saxon layout. This was the road
leading into the city from the north—Widemarsh Street. By

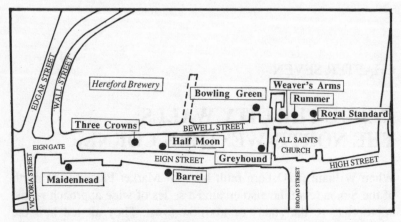

comparison with the other approach roads, it is narrow throughout its length and enters, rather apologetically, into the western end of the market place. Before the Conquest it would have led to the Saxon north gate, in front of All Saints Church; at an even earlier date it may have taken a winding course down to a ford crossing of the Wye.

For well over a hundred years the new Norman town was completely undefended. The Saxon works had fallen into disrepair to such an extent that Hereford was described by William of Malmesbury about 1125 as 'not large, but such as appeared by the ruins of broken ditches to have been something great'. It was King Richard I who gave the citizens the right and power to enclose their city when he granted them their first Charter in 1189. The burgesses wasted no time. They made use of the old Saxon defensive works on the west of the town and built a new extension to the north to include the whole of the Norman market place and portions of the grand approach roads. The castle provided all the defence that was needed on the east.

The new enclosure consisted of a ditch and embankment, probably with a strong fence of brushwood and thorn palings on the summit. Gates had to be built where the defensive line crossed the main roads—Eign Gate, Widemarsh Gate, Bye Street Gate, St.

Owen's Gate in the new works, and Friars' Gate as a replacement for the original Saxon west gate. Whilst the enthusiasm was there the work on the new defences proceeded quite quickly, but the replacement of the embankment with a stone wall took much longer and it was not until 1265 that the whole project was completed. Hereford was then as strong a walled town as any in England.

Inside the walls, the principal roads leading towards the market place were where many of the important city hotels and inns could be found. Eign Street, now confusingly called Eign Gate, together with Bewell Street was the western entry and both streets had their share of inns. Just inside Eign Gate, which was demolished in 1787, and on the southern side of the street, was the **Maidenhead Inn**. On its western side was Gunners Lane, a narrow passage which ran between the city wall and the **Maidenhead**, joining Eign Street to West Street. Until the 1880's there was no access from West Street into Victoria Street, for one of the semi-circular towers belonging to the city wall sealed the street and Gunners Lane was then the only way out. With the present Inner Relief Road, the problem is much the same, and Gunners Lane still serves pedestrians well, although now it is principally used as access to the subway.

The Maidenhead a few years after closure

83

The **Maidenhead** is of considerable antiquity and was advertised to be let in 1775 after which William Turner took over as landlord.

Inns such as this were often used for auction sales—the bids inevitably came a little more easily after the customer had had a few drinks! Thus there was advertised:

Freehold Property

to be sold by Auction

by W.M. James

at the Maidenhead Inn

on Thursday the 31st day of October 1839,

at five o'clock in the afternoon

in one or more lots.

All those Eight newly built substantial Brick-built Dwelling Houses known as Moorfield Row, near Eign Gate, in this City

The **Maiden Head**, as it was described from time to time, eventually became part of the Imperial Brewery empire and, at the time of the sale in 1898, it provided an income of £42 of which £12 was from the stabling. It then had 'a Lofty Bar with Two Entrances, Smoke Room, Billiard Room with Bar, Jug and Bottle, Entrance, Back Kitchen, Sitting Room, Kitchen, Store Room, Nine Bed Rooms, large Sitting Room, Five Attics and small Yard.' It was taken over by the Hereford and Tredegar Brewery and they carried out extensive alterations in 1900 to provide a larger billiard room, a bowling alley and additional letting bedrooms. By 1907, the billiard room had been extended again indicating the growing popularity of the game, and part of the ground floor had become a 'Public Luncheon Bar'. There were still extensive stables and a coach house at the rear with access from West Street.

In October 1909, the **Maidenhead** had a change of name and become the slightly more posh **Eigne Gate Hotel**. The change must not have been a success for the inn closed in 1925. Four years later the property was described in the Directory as 'Fred Chard, draper and Post Office', but by the beginning of the war the building had been taken over by Jessons Army and Navy Stores. It still functions with the same family name over 50 years later.

On the opposite side of the street and a little nearer the centre of the city, the **Three Crowns** has, at the time of writing, been empty for some two years. The inn continued through from Eign Street to

Bewell Street, where there was a rear entry which at one time led directly into the public bar. Throughout the second half of the 19th century this rear entry may well have had a greater use than the

Waiting outside the rear of the Three Crowns in Bewell Streeet

front door, for across Bewell Street and directly opposite this door was the main entry into the Hereford Brewery.

The earliest reference to the **Three Crowns** is in 1831, when John Woodyatt was landlord. However, in 1779 there was advertised 'The Sign of the **Three Horse Shoes Inn** in Eygne Street, a well-accustomed house with good stabling and cellaring, situate near Eygne gate, the entrance to this city from the principal parts of South Wales'. There is also an even earlier reference to the **Three Blackbirds** in the same area. The **Three Horse Shoes** is mentioned again in 1796 and 1804 and the 'Alehouse Keepers' Recognizance' for 1826 describes the premises as 'the **Three Crowns** (late the **Three Horse Shoes**)'. Was three the magic number for this inn, changing from Blackbirds to Horseshoes and finally to Crowns to suit different landlords?

It was apparently to become the landlord of the **Three Crowns** that Charles Watkins came to Hereford as a single man in the early 1840's. He soon married Ann Hill and, by 1850, had moved to the **Imperial** in Widemarsh Street. However, he continued to have an interest in the **Three Crowns** and was still shown as landlord in the 1858 Directory. By this time he had purchased the old Hereford Brewery and renamed it the Imperial Brewery. The Imperial eventually held the freehold of the **Three Crowns**, as it did with many inns in the city and neighbourhood. However, it was not put out as a tenancy, as was normal, but was kept under management.

When the inn was sold in 1898, at the same time as the brewery, it included, in addition to a long bar, smoke room and private parlour, a brick and tiled building at the rear which contained the workmen's allowance room and two hop rooms, all used in connection with the brewery. It is only to be expected that the brewery employees would frequent the public bar of the inn on their doorstep; the inn where they collected their allowance.

The **Three Crowns** continued with its large and high public bar and its small snug or smoke room well into the 1980's, but it eventually succumbed to the modern need for a single, large, open space and the ground floor was completely revamped so that internally it looked like any other pub of the period, designed principally to serve meals to businessmen at lunchtime.

A few doors nearer to the centre of the city was the Head Office and Retail Stores for the Imperial Brewery. Although only used as offices and stores, it was fully licensed as the **Half Moon Inn** in the 1870's, having been an inn in its own right in 1858 when it was known as the **Dolphin**. This was a freehold property belonging to the Brewery, but for some reason was subject to an Annual Chief Rent of 1s. 4¹/2d. payable to the Ecclesiastical Commissioners and an Annual Fee Farm Rent of 6d. payable to the Town Council. The ground floor contained a counting house, order office and the retail wine and spirit department, whilst upstairs were storerooms and the owners' private office. As late as 1950, when the building was the wine and spirit stores for the Hereford, Tredegar and Cheltenham Brewery, Ltd., it was also entered in the Directory as the **Half Moon** Public House. The licence was finally surrendered in the early 1960's when a new off-licence was granted in its place.

Almost opposite the brewery offices was a 17th century timber-framed building with two gables on the front. According to Collins this building was once the town residence of a county magnate, and it does not appear as an inn in the 1858 Directory or on the map of the same date. However, it is recorded in 1822 under the name of the **Wine Vaults**. This was the same building that was for sale by auction in August, 1841, described as: 'All that Messuage, or Tenement and Inn, called "**No. 12**", situate in Eign Street, together with garden, yard, stable, coach-house and other convenient buildings at the back thereof, communicating with Packer's Lane, and now in the occupation of Mr. William Lloyd.'

The Barrel in the late 1930's

The main business was apparently the Wine and Spirit trade and in the 1891 directory it was still described as **No. 12, Wine and Spirit Vaults**, then belonging to the Tewkesbury Brewery Company. By 1905 the **Vaults** belonged to the more familiar Arnold, Perrett & Co. who had offices at the **White Hart** in Broad Street, and in later directories it is always shown simply as the **Barrel Inn**.

The **Barrel** was next door to the recently-closed Jennings Saddlers and Sports Shop, being one further away from town. Alwyne Arthur Davies became the landlord just before the Second World War, and only narrowly escaped with his life when the pub was completely burnt out in 1942. The site remained vacant for several years and even now the replacement building has a temporary air about it, as though waiting for the **Barrel** to be restored.

One inn which is the cause of some confusion is the **New City Arms** which, at the end of the 18th century and through until the middle of the 19th century, was in Eign Street. It was recorded as such in 1792, whilst in May 1835 there was offered to let: 'All that well-accustomed Public House, with stabling etc, Situate in Eign Street in the City and known by the Sign of the **New City Arms** now in the possession of John Overton. An active industrious tenant will meet with every encouragement and will not be required to take any stock in trade'. Described as having an access to Bewell Street, this must have been one of the properties on the north side of Eign Street. It is not mentioned in 1872—could it have changed its name to the **Leg of Mutton**, recorded then in Eign Street, only to change its name once more in 1874 to the **Anchor Dining Rooms** and close shortly afterwards?

There was yet another public house in the part of Eign Street within the Gate. This was the **Greyhound Hotel** which was only separated from All Saints Church by the narrow Cross Street, or All Saints Passage as it is now known. The **Greyhound Hotel** was certainly in existence in 1826 when it was run by John Taylor and Elizabeth Lane. Towards the end of that century alterations were carried out to modernise the building. The work included the insertion of a bathroom on the first floor and toilets on both first and second floors. At that time it had fourteen letting bedrooms. On the ground floor an opening led from Bewell Street into a small yard.

The scullery and kitchen were on one side and the stock room on the other. More or less central to the building, with an entrance from the back passage, was the public bar with a small parlour between it and Cross Street. To the left of the front entrance was a coffee room and on the right the commercial room.

The variety and the uses of the various rooms shows that the inn was very typical of its day; a brick-built hotel, well-placed in the centre of the town. But underneath it are the remains of a much earlier building. According to William Collins, the inn was established in 1673 on the site of the refectory of the Master and Brethren of the Hospital at Vienne, in Dauphiné, which was given by Henry III, in 1249, and confirmed by Edward I in 1296. Watkins refers to it as the Hospital of St. Anthony which was closely connected with All Saints Church.

Underneath what was the bar and the small parlour, is a medieval, vaulted chamber which, according to the Hereford architect, Edward J. Bettington, who surveyed it in 1932, originally extended south across the full width of Eign Street. The medieval cellar is some 22 feet long and 13 feet wide with groined and arched recesses on the north and east sides. The only access is from the front cellar, through a doorway and down five steps. In the front cellar there is a stone fireplace probably of a somewhat later date than the chamber. The floor of the front cellar is about 7 feet below the outside pavement, the medieval one is some 3^1/2 feet lower. As with several other early cellars in Hereford, it does not relate in any way to the building above. The latter merely made use of the cellar walls as foundations when the earlier, above-ground portions of the buildings were swept away. The recesses suggest that the original use of the building was for storage, but that use probably changed when the fireplace was inserted in the front cellar. By that time it may have been in use as a tavern with a stepped entry from the street. It is extremely unlikely that the cellars ever continued all the way across Eign Street as suggested by Bettington, and equally unlikely that there was ever a direct communication between the cellars and a postulated crypt underneath the western part of All Saints Church.

At the turn of the century, the **Greyhound** was one of the smartest hotels in the city, catering for the county gentry and commercial visitors. Here, county teams put up in the early days of cricket. The **Greyhound** ceased trading in 1924 and then became a drapers shop—Messrs. Witts and Cole. In recent years it was a branch of Burton's menswear and is now called Kutz. The medieval cellar, although no longer used, still survives underneath the shop.

The rest of the inns which existed in this part of the city were all in the narrow Bewell Street which runs parallel to and just to the north of Eign Gate Street. Much of this street is now the home of a Tesco supermarket, but in the 19th century it was a thriving street of houses, inns and shops, with a series of 'courts' such as Sheriffs Court and Fryers Court leading off to the north and containing small, half-timbered houses, long since demolished as part of a slum clearance scheme. Towards the western end of the street was Bewell House, built as a town house for a Monmouthshire squire. It adjoined, and eventually became part of, the Hereford Brewery which, under various names, was an important industry in Hereford from its start in 1834 until its final demolition in the early 1960's.

The well-used back door of the **Three Crowns** was opposite the Brewery and, a few yards further along the street, on the Brewery side, the **Bowling Green Inn** still survives. Behind it, the bowling green is claimed to be one of the oldest in the country, possibly laid out as early as 1484. Bowls was certainly being played in Hereford in the early part of the 16th century, but the first specific mention of the green as such is in 1697. The **Bowling Green** was also the place to play billiards, for as early as 1662 John Cole was presented for the offence of keeping a billiard table.

It was at the **Bowling Green** that the earliest Friendly Society in Hereford was formed. This was in 1766, but the members eventually moved to the **Green Dragon** where they stayed for many years. The inn was also the home for the Palladian Lodge of the Masons, which was founded there in 1762. Slightly more worrying to some of the populace of Hereford would have been the 'Society for the Prosecution of Felons', founded at the inn in 1824.

It was in 1834 that William Radford decided to build an iron foundry in Friar Street. Radford was an ex-sea captain who had been building boats for use on the Wye for several years. He was a lover of the spectacular, and had just launched his steamer, the 80ft. long Water Witch, from his yard. There were eighty people on board and he arranged for the bells of St. Nicholas Church to ring out! To celebrate the start of his new enterprise in Friar Street, he organised a procession, led by a band, which started at the **Bowling Green**. It went to the building site to deliver the plans to the contractor and then returned to the inn, full of thirst, for an evening's jollification.

The Bowling Green before it was set back from the street

Originally, the whole property was quite extensive including not only the green and the present clubhouse, but also the premises next

door. In 1836, Joseph Powell took over the inn and, in announcing the event, indicated that 'Strict attention to the wants, comfort and amusement of his customers, will, he trusts, entitle him to a share of their favours.' Perhaps his customers were not prepared to grant him any favours at all, for he left within a year! He was followed by a Mr. R. Williams who instigated a series of Bowling Green Dinners which were served at 3 o'clock. By December, 1839, Mr. Williams had left and the new landlord, E.S. Jones was inviting 'his friends and the public generally to a Housewarming Dinner' for which tickets 'including waiters' were available at five shillings and six pence. Mr. Jones was much more unlucky than his two predecessors for a month later, in January 1840, the inn was advertised by his assignees as being 'to let, with immediate possession.' The potential was apparently there, for the premises were described as 'having lately been very much improved at a great expense and are rendered capable of carrying on one of the first businesses in Town.' Just over a month later the furniture was sold by auction and in March the inn was advertised yet again:

'To be Let with immediate possession that old establishment called the **Bowling Green**, the whole of which has been recently altered and considerably improved. The Premises next the street comprises a front Parlour with cellar underneath, Inner Bar, Kitchen and five bedrooms above. Fronting the Green, a newly-erected Smoking Room, the best in Hereford; Billiard Room, with an excellent Table complete; a spacious Dining Room and Ante-room; and commodious Vaulted cellarage under the whole; Brewhouse with new Coppers, and every Brewing requisite.

'The **Bowling Green** is ornamented with well fitted-up alcoves, and surrounded by a most productive garden, walled in, and well planted with choice Fruit Trees, in a full state of bearing. Excellent skittle ground, fenced off. The whole of the lower rooms are furnished ... and the premises, which form one of the most pleasant and healthful residences in the City, will be let at a very moderate rent.'

The sale included an additional billiard table and a 'fine-toned organ, well adapted for a small church or chapel', both of which were apparently on the premises. The bowling green and the rear building tended to operate as a private club and, by the mid-19th century the clubhouse was known as 'Albert's Billiard Rooms'.

The whole property was sold in 1877, when John Wright was tenant at an annual rent of £45 per annum. It was again on the market in 1896, when it was held by Messrs. Arnold, Perrett & Co. They had a full repairing lease expiring in 1902 at an annual rent of £70. Charles George Errington, who was the landlord, was also manager of the Dining Rooms which were next door. At that time the bowling green was described as 'one of the largest and best kept in the West of England'. Was this why the Bowling Club won all their home matches in 1901 and had a visit from a New Zealand team the following year?

The **Bowling Green** was eventually bought by Messrs. Flower & Sons, brewers of Stratford on Avon, who built the lean-to extension on the front of the Clubhouse in 1903. A serious situation developed in 1912, when the magistrates challenged the renewal of the licence for the inn, because they considered that the premises were structurally unsafe, the rooms were small, and the ventilation poor. At that time the City Council had a scheme to widen Bewell Street by seventeen feet and, like many such schemes, this one effectively put a blight on the whole area. However, it allowed the brewery to blame the City Council for their lack of maintenance. They even went as far as putting forward proposals to reconstruct the inn and the shop next door, which they then also owned, with a frontage set back some 17 feet from the edge of the road. The new building was designed by James Villat of Cheltenham, but it was apparently not built until the 1930's. The half-timbered facade was set back by the required seventeen feet to await the new, broad thoroughfare but, like many other grand schemes, nothing happened. Bewell Street has continued as a narrow back lane with the **Bowling Green** and the Bowling Club at its rear as a visible reminder of what was a bustling community at the turn of the century.

A couple of doors further up Bewell Street, and directly opposite the tower of All Saints Church was the **Weaver's Arms**. This was a typical, small, back-street inn containing a minute, stand-up bar, 8 feet wide and 4 feet deep and a larger room, which was dignified as a smoke room on plans produced in 1901 by the Tredegar and Hereford Brewery. Although the plans envisaged new toilets in the yard at the rear, the building was too small to survive as an inn, being only 16 feet square, and in 1903 the licence was not renewed.

Two doors past the **Weaver's Arms** and the determined pub crawler in the late 19th century Bewell Street could fall into the **Rummer Tavern**. Perhaps he even drank out of a 'rummer'—the large drinking glass, after which the inn was named. The **Rummer Tavern** was in existence at the beginning of the 19th century when it was the home of one of the less expensive of the friendly societies. In the yard behind the inn was a large boiler which, for many years, was used for making tallow candles, much used for illumination in the 19th century. In 1836, the landlord was the same E.S. Jones who, three years later, was to move to the **Bowling Green**. In advertising his arrival at the **Rummer**, he advised all his customers that he would continue to 'tune Piano Fortes, and to form Quadrille Bands on the shortest notice', so it would appear that he viewed the inn as not being a full time job. Some six months after Mr. Jones' arrival, an auction was held in the 'Great Room' in the inn of '100 dozen of prime-crusted old port wine and about 100 gallons of very superior Pale Sherry Wine now in the Wood', all without reserve.

This was the period when public exhibitions of all kinds were acceptable. The landlord of the **Rummer** advertised one such 'Extraordinary and Pleasing Exhibition' in the *Hereford Times* occurring 'each day from 12 in the morning to 10 at night' when a Mr. Ledgwood, who had been 'born without hands or arms, and with only one leg and foot would in the acquirements of Art and Education, display various specimens of his ingenuity.'

The inn was put up for sale by auction in 1898. Even then, the auctioneer was pointing out the difficulty in obtaining good licensed property, due to the large brewing firms 'absorbing them into their concessions'. At that time it was described as having a good bar, tap room and smoke room on the ground floor, with a club room and six good bedrooms. An adjoining warehouse, which had been used as an ironmongers store, was part of the property. The sale was not particularly successful for within a short length of time the building had been converted to a lodging house and the licence was lost.

Our conscientious Victorian boozer had not yet finished with the north side of Bewell Street, for all that separated the **Rummer Tavern** from the **Royal Standard** was the Foresters Hall! When advertised for sale in 1889, the **Royal Standard** was described as: 'A free, full licensed public house, number 43 Bewell Street, near the city centre and the markets ... The House is brick and timber built and is one of the oldest licensed houses in the city; it comprises, cellar, bar, bar-parlour, smoke room, kitchen, pantry, and six bedrooms. The buildings at the rear are brick built, and include Brewhouse, coalhouse, two W.C.'s and urinal with brick paved yard'. It had been an inn in 1826 and probably much earlier.

The **Royal Standard** survived for quite a while after its smaller and less historic neighbours had closed, but it eventually ceased to operate as a licensed premises in 1922. The various parts of the building must have been split up into different tenancies for in the 1929 Directory number 43 Bewell Street included Mrs. Susan Cook, a second-hand clothes dealer; Peter O'Hare, a scrap metal merchant; Mrs. T. Vale, a greengrocer; and Fred Underwood, who operated a fried fish shop!

CHAPTER EIGHT

WIDEMARSH STREET WITHIN THE GATE

The narrow Widemarsh Street runs from the western edge of High Town, crossing the Inner Relief Road where Widemarsh Gate used to stand and then heading north towards Leominster and Ludlow. Narrow as it is now, this does not compare with the earlier part of the 19th century when many of the properties on the eastern side towards High Town included basement entries from the street. These open areas, which also provided some illumination for the cellars underneath the buildings, would have been railed off from the street. At some long-forgotten time, the then City Council must have decreed that these areas should be sealed over to provide a footpath and allow the road to be widened. They still remain hidden underneath the pavement from High Town almost as far as Maylord Street, giving rise to the stories of underground passages in this area.

The eastern side of the part of Widemarsh Street that is inside the Relief Road has suffered little change in the last 100 years or so as far as the actual buildings are concerned, but the uses to which these buildings are now put has inevitably altered. There are now no inns at all, but in the late 19th century there were several including the two which were curiously named simply **No. Five** and **No. Ten**. In the late nineteenth century it was relatively easy to obtain licenses to brew beer. Because of this, during the peak periods licences for Beer-houses were often issued to numbered houses, some of which did not bother to name their premises.

This may not have been the explanation in Hereford, for **No. Five** was the public house nearest to High Town and was actually

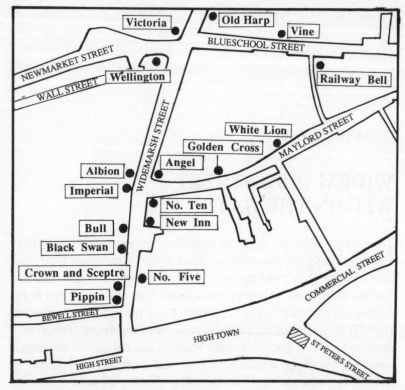

number 148 Widemarsh Street. The street was renumbered some years ago and, as this was the 'evens' side, the building then, rather confusingly, ended up as number 10. It is assumed that it was originally called **No. Five** because it was half way between the High Town corner and **No. Ten**.

George Townsend moved from premises in Church Street to take up the management of **No. Five, Wine and Spirit Vaults** in July 1841. It had been a public house for some time before that date with Daniel Herbert as tenant. He had moved just up the street to the **New Inn**. Townsend took rapid action and by November of that year he was able to advertise:

'In returning thanks for the liberal encouragement he has been favoured with since his commencement in the above grog shop and tavern, respectfully acquaints the Public generally, that in addition to the Wine and Spirit Trade, he has opened a Brewery, where families may be supplied on the shortest notice in any quantity,

No.5

with good wholesome Home-Brewed, of any strength, in Casks or Bottles.'

He advertised his prices, his 'fine ale' being one shilling a gallon. At that time the cost of the bottles was of considerable significance and his prices for wines and spirits did not include the container.

Port and sherry varied from 36 shillings to 48 shillings a dozen according to quality although a 'Superior Old Cape' could be obtained for 24 shillings. Sparkling Champagne was 8 shillings for a quart bottle. Spirits varied from 32 shillings for a gallon of 'Superior Old French Brandy' to as little as 10 shillings and 8 pence for a gallon of his cheapest 'Fine London Gin'. The Brewery could have been at the back of the property, but there is no surviving evidence.

In February 1849, Townsend advertised a consignment of Irish XX Stout, which he had obtained direct from Dublin. He used the opportunity to thank 'his friends and fellow citizens, for their kind assistance during the late fire, by which it was prevented extending to his premises.' At some time later in the century **No. Five** was taken over by Charles Watkins and Son, but it did not appear in the list of hotels in the grand Brewery sale of 1898 so must have been sold on again before that date.

The cellar underneath **No. Five** would have been in use throughout the life of the inn and apparently had an access from the rear as well as the roadside entry. It is part of a complex of cellars which belong to properties which front the western part of High Town and the southern part of Widemarsh Street. None are used now, but during the Second World War they were collectively pressed into service as a large air raid shelter with an entry through **No. Five**. It would appear that there was another entry within the Butter Market, where a sign still survives.

No. Five continued as a public house until 1957 after which it became for a time a free library and then the more well-known Dolls Hospital. It is now a shop, but the fine three-storey facade is well composed and looks as though it was copied straight out of a neo-classical pattern book. The only compromise to the regular design was the ground-floor passage entry which led to the inn yard and to the rear of several other properties in the area. The rear part of the building is slightly earlier than the rest and probably dates to the early 19th century. The frontage building was built in the third quarter of that century, possibly when it became part of the Watkins empire.

No. Ten was the new name for the historic **New Inn** after it fell on hard times. The original **New Inn** must have occupied the whole of the corner of Widemarsh Street and Maylord Street, with an extensive frontage to the former and a large courtyard along the latter. The courtyard joined that of the **Redstreak Tree** which stretched through from High Town. In 1809 both inns were bought by the Corporation to provide land on which to build a Council Chamber, a Guildhall, and a poultry and butter market. The front part of the **New Inn** was then converted into a Common Council Room and the great room behind it into a Guildhall for the City Courts. The Butter Market, with accesses from High Town, Widemarsh Street and Maylord Street, was opened in 1816. The inn is shown on the 1885 Ordnance Survey map as being between the Vegetable Market (which was on the corner of Maylord and Widemarsh Streets) and the passageway that provided joint access from Widemarsh Street to the Butter Market and to the inn yard. The Guildhall is shown on that map as being at the rear of the shops to the south of the passageway. The 1858 map has a similar arrangement, but shows a flight of stairs leading from the open Butter Market into the 1885 Guildhall. Was the Council Chamber actually in the basement, as suggested by William Collins in his *Historical Landmarks of Hereford*, until it was moved a storey higher in 1862-3?

In 1840, George Weaver was landlord of the **New Inn** and could offer 'well-aired beds, capital stabling, lock-up coach houses etc.' so some grounds were still attached to the inn. The following year it was taken over by Daniel Herbert who also described himself as the sole agent for the rather doubtful sounding 'Bett's Patent Brandy'. He had moved from No. 5 and described the new premises as being 'more extensive and convenient'. Towards the end of the decade, Edward Fowles took over the house and proceeded to change its image. It rapidly became the **New Inn & Commercial Hotel** and there were regular advertisements in the *Hereford Times*:

February 5th 1848: 'Grand Scheme
All the Money Divided !!!
208 Prizes !!!
Derby Venture !!!'

And, a month later:

'constantly on hire Phaetons, Gigs and Horses, in excellent condition, and at reasonable prices . .'

And in November, still looking for additional trade, he made use of Rowland Hill's penny post:

'E. Fowles will be happy on application to forward free through the post, to any part of the country, a copy of his MODUS OPERANDI on receipt of a stamped envelope, superscribed with the address of the applicant.'

It was some time during the third quarter of the 19th century that the **New Inn** became **No. 10**. This was not a quirk of the house numbering in Widemarsh Street, for the street number of the establishment is given in the Directories of the period as number 142. A careful examination of the detailed Ordnance Survey plan of 1885 provides the clue to the new name, if not the reason for the change. Counting individual properties northwards from High Town, the **New Inn** was the tenth property along the street. Inevitably, **No. Five** was the fifth property. Was this numbering to aid the slightly drunken visitor to Hereford finding his way back to his hotel by counting individual doorways along the dark streets?

No. Ten did not survive as long as **No. Five** for it fell into the clutches of the Licensing Committee in 1919. Compensation was agreed in the sum of £1,100 and the license was extinguished. The site is now occupied by an electricity showroom.

The Angel Inn—Garrick's birth place

A little further up Widemarsh Street and on the opposite corner of Maylord Street to the **New Inn,** was another historic tavern with an equally complex series of name changes. This was the **Angel Inn**, a twin-gabled, half-timbered building of three full stories, with attic space above and extensive cellars below. It was here, in 1717, that David Garrick, the great English actor was born. His father, Captain Peter Garrick, was probably stationed in Hereford, and had made arrangements for his wife, Arabella, to stay at the **Angel** where she gave birth to her son. He was baptised in All Saints Church a few days later, but then left Hereford for future fame and fortune.

The **Angel** was destroyed by fire early in the 19th century and was rebuilt as two separate properties which were described in 1881 as 'A messuage, Dwelling House and Inn being 139 Widemarsh Street and Known as The **Raven Inn** and in the occupation of Mr George Horne, Brewer, and A Messuage, Dwelling House and Shop adjoining the above and being part in Widemarsh Street and part in Maylord Street being 140 Widemarsh Street and recently in the occupation of Mr Hodges, Hairdresser and now void.' These were the two properties that had been bought for £1,170 by a Mr. T. Showell from a Mr. Powell, who lived in Adelaide in Australia. Mr Showell had to obtain mortgages to buy the properties and, by 1886, had become heavily in debt. Presumably this Mr. Showell had nothing to do with Showell's Brewery Company of Birmingham that owned the **Crown** in St. Martin's Street early in the 20th century! The properties were eventually sold by the mortgagees to Philip Ballard, described as a Gentleman of The Knoll, Tupsley, for £1,645. There were some changes—the inn had changed its name and become the **Garrick's Head** in the occupation of Charles Perkins, and the shop was occupied by Bell & Co., Butchers. The inn name, which had been entered in the Directory for 1885 as the **Garrick Vaults**, did not last for long. In 1888 the whole property was again for sale. It included 139, once again called the **Raven**, and described as being in Widemarsh Street and Maylord Street, and the corner shop adjoining. They were to be sold by direction of Stephen and Thomas Ballard, younger brother and nephew respectively of the late Philip Ballard.

Stephen Ballard was the enthusiastic clerk to the Herefordshire and Gloucestershire Canal Company who had been instrumental in

completing the canal to Hereford by 1845. His elder brother, Philip, who was born in 1800, was manager of the canal from its opening in 1845 until its final closure in 1883. He retired to his home, The Knoll at Tupsley, and was murdered there on the night of 24th October 1887. The two men who were eventually hung for the crime achieved such notoriety that they were modelled in wax at Madame Tussauds.

The 1888 sale details indicate that the landlord of the **Raven** was a Mr. Eli Smith, and that the corner shop was then occupied by the American Meat Company. Eli Smith bought the buildings for

£1,200, but eleven months later sold them to Arnold, Perrett & Co. for £3,150—a remarkable profit in less than a year!

By 1891, the **Raven** was entered in the Directory as 1 Maylord Street, with Robert Jollow as landlord. It is evident that the new owners had remodelled the whole building to become a single unit. It continued as an inn throughout the first half of the 20th century, and towards the end of its life was much frequented by gypsies. It had a reputation for horse dealing and allied activities and was known as a good place for a fight on a Saturday night. Its final closure was in 1959 when the licence was surrendered in favour of a full 'On Licence' to replace the existing 'Beer On' at the **Sawyer's Rest** in Burcott Road.

Bulmers Vaults; later The Pippin

The western side of Widemarsh Street contained a wide variety of public houses and hotels, the nearest one to the centre of the city being on the corner of Bewell Street. This was no. 2 Widemarsh Street (now no. 3) which, in 1826 and for many years thereafter, was simply known as the **Wine Vaults**. It became John and William Bulmer's wine and spirit merchants, known locally as **Bulmers Vaults**, and in 1969 was renamed **The Pippin**. The sign refers to apples of various varieties such as the Wyken Pippin, and is very appropriate in this cider-producing area. During its last few years the **Pippin** belonged to Ansells Brewery and was eventually closed and sold by auction in 1984 for £176,000. It is now a shop.

The fifteenth century cellars underneath The Pippin

The **Pippin** is a rather fine three-storey building on an important corner site and was built about 1790 to the design of William Parker, who was also responsible for the oldest part of the General Hospital. Was it Parker or his unknown client who insisted that the cellars of the previous building should be preserved underneath the new one? Hidden beneath the present shop and extending underneath the property to the north are a range of 15th century cellars with four-centred, barrel-vaulted roofs made of squared stone. They contain arched doorways and a window which still has its original iron bars. In the ceiling are stone panels carved with foliated designs and shields which appear to be merchants marks. It is a great pity that these fine cellars cannot be brought back into a beneficial use which would allow them to be seen and properly appreciated.

Just to the north of the **Pippin**, at no. 5, was the **Crown and Sceptre** which was advertised in the *Hereford Journal* as being for sale in 1780. Almost half a century later the same paper advertised an auction 'On the premises of Mr. James Davies of the **Crown and Sceptre** Inn in Widemarsh Street on Tuesday the 3rd Day of October, 1826, and the following days under an execution in the office of sheriff, all the valuable stock in trade, consisting of upwards of 6,000 gallons of ale and strong beer, spirits, malt, hops, etc. Together with all household furniture, brewing utensils and other effects.' The surprisingly large amount of ale in stock was possibly due to the practice of allowing the ale and beer to mature before sale, or because of the extensive off sales from the premises. It was some four years later that a Daniel Davies, presumably a relative of the unfortunate James, advertised that 'in consequence of the great increase in his wine and spirit business he is compelled to discontinue the **Crown and Sceptre** as an Inn or Public House, from and after the 2nd January 1831'.

The wine and spirit sales must have been a friendly business for he completed his advertisement with: 'Persons at any time wishing to indulge themselves with a glass of excellent wine, spirits or grog, may rely on being comfortably accommodated at No. 5 Widemarsh Street'. He must have anticipated substantial off-sales as a result!

The cellars previously described as being underneath nos 1-4 Widemarsh Street, may have continued underneath no. 5. They were also examined by Mr. E.J. Bettington about 1937 who found 'a place for storing wines, etc, cupboards and shelves' and a blocked 14th century doorway leading to no. 4. There is still a blocked doorway in no. 4 but the cellars of no. 5 were filled in when the first part of the Co-op was built. Mr. Bettington thought that the cellars may have continued through as far as the **Black Swan**, the next building to the north.

The **Black Swan Hotel** was a courtyard inn which was demolished in 1978, despite local and national protests, to make way for a

The Black Swan shortly before demolition

Job Centre that was never built. The site remained vacant for over a decade before being taken over by the Co-op who then extended their small store at nos. 5 & 6 to cover the whole site.

The earliest mention of the **Black Swan** is in 1663, when the landlord was Thomas Prise, but the timber-framed inn had been built a little earlier in that century. In 1712 the landlord had the delightful name of William Light-holder, but by 1752 Thomas Churchill was mine host. At that time the inn had stabling for 80 horses and was one of the principal hotels in the city. Profits must have been excellent for an extension was built onto the rear and the

Part of the courtyard of the Black Swan before demolition

timber-framed facade was replaced with a fashionable brick front and a driving-way was made through to the inn courtyard.

In 1834 a daily coach called 'The Protector' left the **Black Swan** at 5.45 a.m. to arrive in Liverpool by 6.45 p.m. Stage Wagons, carrying heavy goods, also used the inn as a base; by 1835 one went via Worcester (for the canal to Birmingham and the north) to the Bell Inn in Warwick Lane, London. By 1835, there was a daily coach for London, which left at 4.45 a.m. every morning except Sunday.

The inn was for sale the following year:

'All that substantial messuage or Dwelling-house, with excellent Cellaring, extensive stabling, Coach-houses and every other requisite for carrying on a highly respectable business, called or known by the name of the **Black Swan and Leominster Hotel**, most desirably situate in Widemarsh Street, in the city of Hereford and now in the occupation of Mr. John Humphrey.

'The above premises are in complete repair; a very excellent and improving business is being carried on there; and as regards accommodation, this Inn may be regarded as one of the finest Commercial and Agricultural Inns in the Country.'

Mr. Humphrey was an energetic landlord—in 1839 he held his 'Annual Dinner' on the 23rd January (Gentlemen's Dinner Tickets

3s. 6d.), and five days later had his 'Annual Card and Dancing Assembly'. Dancing was to start at eight o'clock and tickets were 4s. for ladies but 7s. for gentlemen!

Auctions were regular events and could include property—the Nelson Inn at Bishopstone was sold there in 1840—or fine wines: 'Eight Dozen Marsala; fifty-three dozen Sherry, twenty-four dozen Port (1830 & 1832 vintages)—Samples drawn at three, sale at four o'clock, in the Billiard Room'—were sold in 1841. The inn was sufficiently respectable for the City Council to meet there whilst their Council Chamber was being altered in 1862.

Although the **Black Swan** must have lost some trade following the arrival of the railway, it continued to have a solid local use and early in the twentieth century a new dining hall, some 65 feet long, with its own separate entry from the courtyard, was built above the stables. Unfortunately this was not a success and by 1930 it had been converted to a skittle alley.

It was during 1930 that proposals were put forward by the Cheltenham Brewery Company, who then owned the building, to convert the public bar, which had been in the roadside part of the inn, into two shops. The coffee room and dining room on the first floor above the proposed shops were to become stock rooms. When the application came before the magistrates, the chief constable objected. He pointed out that the new bar and the smoke room, both in the rear part of the building, 'would be concealed from police observation by the closing of the big doors at the street entrance of the hotel and that would not be desirable'. However, the plans were eventually approved and the two shops, one for the Excelsior Meat Company and the other for the Salop, West Midland & Welsh Counties Savings Bank were constructed and opened. After the war, the latter became The Beauty Parlour. A third shop, to the south of the passage, had been there for many years and in the 1960's was the home of Matthew's Tudor Bakery.

In the early 1970's the inn and shops stood vacant for a considerable time whilst negotiations for the retention of the building took place. Eventually, to defeat Civic Trust pickets, demolition commenced early one Sunday morning and by the end of the day the main part of the **Black Swan** had been demolished and one of Hereford's most historic inns had disappeared.

Widemarsh Street also possessed a **White Swan**, mentioned in the will of Elizabeth Russel in 1623. She left the inn to her grand-daughter providing that '52 shillings out of the rents and profits thereof should yerely be given to twelve people of the parish of All Saints.'

A little way beyond the **Black Swan** site is the Mansion House built in 1697 as a town house for Dr. William Brewer. Dr. Brewer bought several properties in Widemarsh Street including a new brick-built house 'formerly the signe of the **Bull** adjoining on the south part to a comon inne called the **Black Swann**.' It would appear that the **Bull** was between the **Swan** and the Mansion House—the building that has, for many years, been the shop of Philip Morris & Son, ironmongers.

The **Imperial Tavern** was originally a long, narrow property with a driving-way on the north side and the Mansion House to the south. It was then no. 12 Widemarsh Street, and it was to this inn that Charles Watkins, the founder of the Imperial Brewery, moved in 1847. As the brewery grew, the **Imperial Vaults** continued under management and in 1898 it had an estimated yearly value of £80. At that time it included a large bar and smoke room but only two bedrooms. It was apparently timber-framed. The rear yard contained the old brewhouse that Charles Watkins had originally used to produce his beer when he bought the inn.

The Albion Hotel, before becoming part of the Imperial Hotel

Next door to it at no. 13 was the short-lived **Albion Hotel**. This rather grand establishment had been built in 1857 by John Clarke Morgan, who had previously been landlord at the **Black Lion** and the **Royal Oak**, both in Wyebridge Street. It did not survive long as a separate inn having been bought out by the Imperial Brewery presumably with the intention of extending the **Imperial**. In 1898 the main part of the building was on a temporary let to a furnishing firm, but the cellars were in use by the **Imperial**. The only way that these cellars could have been used by the **Imperial** would have been by excavating a passage underneath the driving-way which separated the two. The **Albion** was a much larger building than the **Imperial** having spacious living accommodation on the first floor and six bedrooms on the second.

Following the sale in 1898, the two properties came into the possession of Samuel Allsopp and Sons. They employed George Herbert Godsell, a local architect, to combine the two properties into one large inn. His first set of drawings, produced in August 1899, show a rather unhappy attempt to amalgamate the two very different properties. Although it was approved by the then Roads Committee, it was not carried out in practice and in March 1900 Godsell submitted a revised front elevation. The result was effectively a new building, although it reflected the general massing of both earlier properties. The driving-way through the **Albion** was retained and the whole building was provided with what William Collins writing in 1913 saw as 'one of the most beautifully-designed fronts of modern Elizabethan style in the city'.

Without any doubt the **Imperial** is the finest example of vernacular revivalism in Hereford and as such is a great asset to Widemarsh Street. It was opened on Friday 28th June 1901 with Mr. & Mrs. Clay, who had moved from the **Coach & Horses** in Commercial Street, in charge of the new establishment. The cellars belonging to the two earlier buildings continued in use. Because of this a large proportion of the cellarage—that belonging originally to the **Albion**—is underneath the present driving-way. At the rear there were the market room and the stables complete with an extensive loft, a harness room, loose boxes and even a dung bay. The new inn with its large front bar, smoke room approached by a side passage and club room on the first floor, was well-designed for its

The Imperial, with the Mansion House to the left

period. Since then it has had many additions, partitions have been removed between rooms, and has, for many years, been a Berni House. Next door is Saxty's Wine Bar and restaurant, a relatively recent addition to the eating and drinking establishments in Widemarsh Street, but not really a pub.

When the Inner Relief Road was built in 1967 only one inn survived at the junction of Widemarsh Street with Blueschool Street and Newmarket Street. In the nineteenth century this was the **Wellington Arms**, but at a later date it became the **Wellington Hotel**. Until the end of the last century, this old inn stood on the limited piece of ground between the city ditch and the narrow Wall Street, which then continued through into Widemarsh Street. The old timber-framed building sat astride the city wall and had entrances on both sides. It was included in many of the paintings and engravings of Widemarsh Gate, particularly those by James Wathen who produced a series of sketches of the surroundings just before the demolition of the Gate in 1798.

Wathen's sketch of Widemarsh Gate, with the Wellington to the left

The inn survived for another century, but was offered for sale in 1891 with a series of special conditions resulting from the Hereford Improvement Act of 1854. The inn belonged to the City Council and included in the sale was that portion of Wall Street which abutted the inn and led into Widemarsh Street. The purchaser had to demolish the buildings on the western part of the site which were to be replaced with a new section of roadway leading directly into Newmarket Street. The purchaser had also to demolish the whole part of the building which faced into Newmarket Street to provide land on which the Council could widen the street.

The **Wellington** was bought by William Bowers, a builder of Bath Street, for a total of £830. The whole building was eventually demolished, the last part to fall being the section of city wall recorded by Alfred Watkins in a carefully-posed and well-known photograph. A new inn was then built across the line of Wall Street with its front set back to the road improvement line. The abrupt curve at the eastern end of Wall Street, where it joins into the Newmarket Street section of the Inner Relief Road, is well known to all users of the Tesco car park.

The re-built Wellington Hotel

The new **Wellington** continues to serve customers on its corner site next to the Relief Road. It was cleaned recently and now shows its contrasting yellow and red bricks to best effect.

One inn, which is known to have been in this part of Widemarsh Street, has not yet been mentioned. This is the **Black Boy** which was sold by auction to the best bidder on the 26th June 1777. Although present day **Black Boy** inn signs usually depict a young Dickensian chimney sweep the original name would normally have been associated with Negro page-boys. The Hereford inn was described in the sale details as 'A freehold house and cyder house at W'marsh Gate called the **Black Boy** now in the possession of Joseph Partridge ... situate in Bowsey Lane near W'marsh St. (Gate).' The Widemarsh Gate was not pulled down until 1798 and Bowsey Lane was the old name for Wall Street, so it would seem quite likely that the **Black Boy** was the original name of the **Wellington**, changed in 1815 to celebrate the Iron Duke's victory over Napoleon at Waterloo. If this is the case then the **Black Boy** must be the half-timbered building which is shown oversailing the city wall on the views of Widemarsh Gate.

Maylord Street originally went from Widemarsh Street, between the **Angel** on the north and the **New Inn** on the south, in a gentle curve to join Commercial Street just within the city wall line and next to the Bye Street Gate. The eastern part of this street was lost when the Inner Relief Road was built, and it now stops in the centre of the Maylord Orchards development. When it was first built, Maylord Street was the back lane to the long, narrow burgage properties on the northern side of High Town, one of which was the **Redstreak Tree**, the inn that was bought by the Council in 1809 to make way for the Butter Market.

Shortly afterwards, the proprietors of the **Redstreak** apparently took their name to new premises at no. 9 Maylord Street on the opposite side of the street to their old site. Was this a change of name for yet another **Butchers Arms** which was described in 1812 as being near to the back of the new market? It was at the new **Redstreak** that various members of the Bullen family were licensees during the 1830's and '40's. The inn continued to be known as the **Redstreak** or the **Red Streaked Tree** until about 1860 when a Philip Boarse became landlord and changed the name to the more prosaic **Golden Cross.** Its poor position and limited facilities were such that it had comparatively little chance of success. In addition, the new Hereford Times building next door would have towered over it. In 1909 the Licensing Justices refused to renew the licence on the grounds that the house was ill-conducted and it closed as an inn, to re-open as dining rooms a few years later.

The White Lion in Maylord Street

An early inn in Maylord Street is mentioned in various old deeds belonging to the City Council. This was a tenement called **Goodknavesinne** which is specifically mentioned in 1416. It is possible that this was renamed as the **White Lion Inn** which was on the far side of the Hereford Times building and facing Gomond Street. It was in 1759 that the City Corporation 'ordered that whereas the Guildhall is dangerous for the members of this house, future meetings be held at Mr. Newton's, of the **White Lion Inn**, in Bye Street, being the nearest public house to that spot.' Could this have been the Maylord Street **White Lion** just up Gomond Street from the High Town Guildhall?

Described as being well-established in 1856, and with Mr. Thomas Pugh as landlord, the **White Lion** had a 'Brewhouse, Stabling for twenty horses and an arched vault under the same'. Adjoining it, and also in the same sale, was a house, including a walled garden which extended back 'as far as the old town wall'.

It was probably bought by the City Council, for in 1883 they leased it to Thomas Rawlins. After several changes of landlord it was in 1906 or thereabouts that it came into the hands of the Brookes family who eventually bought it. James Brookes was landlord until April, 1920, when he died, but his wife, Mrs. Harriett Brookes, took over and continued to run the inn until she eventually died in May, 1951. Their son Cecil then became licensee until he in turn died in 1966. The Brookes' family had owned and managed the inn for some 60 years.

The **White Lion** was eventually bought by the City Council for a second time in 1967 under a compulsory purchase order. The building was demolished in the same year and a car park took its place. The site is now totally lost within the Maylord Orchard Development.

There have always been inns which served the public for a short length of time then closed down and are rapidly forgotten. One writer mentions two such in the area between Maylord Street and Blueschool Street. They were the **Black Horse** and the **Cherry Tree**; neither are shown on early maps of the city or in the Directories and their precise whereabouts must remain a mystery.

CHAPTER NINE

INSIDE BYE-STREET GATE

Leaving High Town in a north-easterly direction is Commercial Street, once called Bye Street until a misguided Council strove to modernise the city by the cheap expedient of changing the street names. A little way to the east is Union Street, once known as Olde Strete. At Commercial Square, where the Inner Relief Road crosses the junction of Commercial Street and Commercial Road, stood Bye Street Gate—the main entry into the city from Worcester and Bromyard. This was the gate that withstood several sieges until it was successfully taken by Parliamentarian troops in December of 1645. It was demolished in 1798 when it was classified as a 'nuisance' under the terms of the 1774 Paving, Licensing and Lighting Act.

Returning to High Town, the building on the corner of Commercial Street and St. Peter's Street was, until quite recently, an inn. Many people remember the **Tabard**, but do not realise that in historical terms it was relatively new. It occupied a large plot that, until 1863, contained 3 or 4 shops of different ages and sizes. Between 1863 and 1876 the whole area was taken down and rebuilt, more or less as it is now, to become The City and County Dining Rooms. By 1917, the dining function must have decreased a little, for the establishment is entered in the Directory for that year as **City and County Dining Rooms P.H.** It had had an alehouse licence since it opened and effectively by this time it had become a public house with a slightly up-market name. In 1927 this cumbersome name was changed to the **Tabard Inn**, although the name board continued to describe it as an 'Inn and Restaurant'. A tabard

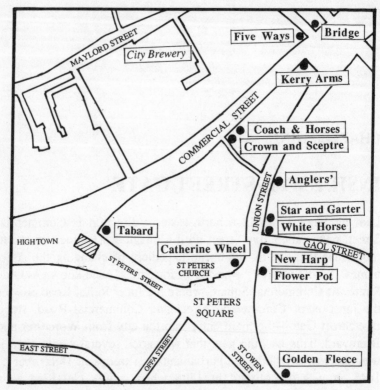

was a garment worn by a knight over his armour, but could also be the sleeveless herald's coat, emblazoned with the arms of the sovereign, that was shown on the Hereford inn sign.

By 1936 the **Tabard** had a Public Bar, Saloon Bar, Lounge and Jug & Bottle—the restaurant had been relegated upstairs. In recent years this was a busy town centre pub—popular at lunchtimes and with a consistent evening trade. It eventually suffered not from a lack of trade, but because of its prime position. It was taken over by the Cheltenham and Gloucester Building Society and eventually, after extensive internal alterations, was opened as their Hereford office.

There were two historic and important inns in Bye Street, both on the southern side and next to each other. The one nearest the centre was the **Crown and Sceptre**. Before about 1840 it was simply the **Crown,** and it was under that name that it was sold in 1831: 'All that well-accustomed public house called the **Crown,** situate in Bye

The Tabard as the City & County Dining Rooms, c. 1911

Street, extending into Union Street, with a malt-house capable of making 1,000 bushels of malt in a season, brew house, cider house, stable yard behind the same, late in the possession of R. Price.' Around 1840, Thomas Cutter was landlord. He was followed by George (Bird) Harding who added the **Sceptre** to the name, possibly in memory of the **Crown and Sceptre** in Widemarsh Street that had closed a few years earlier.

The **Crown and Sceptre** adjoined the narrow passage which still joins Commercial Street and Union Street. Known as Crown Passage in the first half of the 19th century, its name was changed when Richard Morris Harding and Sons took over the inn and converted it into an ironmongers shop in the third quarter of the 19th century. Harding Brothers, as the shop eventually became known, led to the passage being called Harding's Passage for want of a better name. On modern maps it is shown as Union Passage.

Next door to the **Crown** was the **Coach and Horses** which was certainly active at the end of the 18th century and probably much earlier. At that time it was the home of a Friendly Society called the Widow's Club. The members met monthly for eight months of the year and had an annual meeting on the Monday after Midsummer Day. The subscriptions they set were sufficient to allow widows to have a pension of between £10 and £20 per year; and retirement pensions for members over the age of seventy of six shillings a week. Sickness benefit of eight shillings weekly was paid if the member was confined to his room, unless permitted by the doctor to leave it.

In 1887, the Roads Committee approved a scheme for a small spirits vault—effectively a public bar—on the right of the entrance hall. To the left was the coffee room and dining area. In 1890 a hotel bar was built in part of the rear yard. All this work was carried out during the period when Edward Clay was the landlord. At that time the building was a leasehold property of the Hereford Brewery, held for a 14 year term from 11th May 1887. There was also warehousing, stabling and a garden on the opposite side of Union Street. There was little change to the inn during the 1920's— the driving-way into the inn yard from Union Street still had stables and outbuildings surrounding it and apart from the hotel bar there were only two small public rooms, the front bar and the bar parlour. It was, apparently, very popular with the patrons of the adjacent pawnbroker's shop, as they began to liquefy their new assets. Molly Seagar was the well-known barmaid who, with her long golden locks, locally popularised the phrase that 'gentlemen prefer blondes'.

The **Coach and Horses** suffered a name change in 1959 when it became the **Bye Gate Inn**, but as so often happens such a change does not make any difference to the long-term future. This historic inn finally closed in January 1967 and, together with the adjoining Hardings Ironmongers, succumbed to the might of Tesco's who wanted to open what in present day terms was a very small super-market. The new building was hardly a thing of beauty and, of course, Tesco's have moved on. Food and drink are again available, but to a slightly different style, for it is now a branch of Macdonald's.

Bye Street Gate, the largest and most important gate of the city, was probably built during the early part of the 13th century. The buildings associated with the gate included the City Gaol which was demolished in 1842. The gate itself had been demolished at the end of the 18th century, but once both were down, the historic inn on the junction of the two roads was in view to everyone

*The Pack Horse, which was demolished
to make way for the Kerry Arms*

approaching the city. This was then called the **Pack Horse**, but is
now much better known as the **Kerry Arms**.

The **Pack Horse** must be the only inn in the city to have had the
seal of Royal approval by letters patent. The Kerry family were
tavern keepers in the 16th century and possibly earlier. In 1553 an
Act of Parliament limited the number of taverns in each city and
town in the country. Most were limited to one, but Hereford, as an
indication of its importance, was granted the right to have three.
Ale houses, of which there were many, were not affected by this
legislation. The **Pack Horse** had apparently been a tavern, in other
words it sold wine as well as ale, and the landlord would have been
one of the many to suffer from this Act. However, all was not lost
for in 1555, John Kerry became Mayor of Hereford, a position
which then held considerable power. He was an inn-keeper, almost
certainly at the **Pack Horse**, and eventually took matters into his
own hands. He and his wife Johanne petitioned Queen Mary, who
had ascended the throne a few years earlier, to be allowed to re-
open their business as wine-sellers. They received the following
gracious reply:

'Mary by the grace of God, Queen of England, France and Ireland, defender of the faith, to all men to whom these presents shall come greeting.

Whereas by an act of Parliament made in the Parliament held at Westminster the first day of March, in the seventh year of the reign of our most dearest brother King Edward VI., it was amongst other things ordained and provided that no person whatsoever within this realm of England and Wales after the feast of St. Michael the Archangel then next following should keep any tavern, nor sell nor utter by retail any kind of wine to be drunk or spent in his or their mansion-house or other place in their occupation by any colour or means in any city, borough, or town, but only such persons as should be thereto named, appointed, and assigned according to the form and effect of the said act, upon pain of such forfeitures and penalties as in the same act is expressed and contained; Nevertheless as my loving subjects John Kerry, citizen and burgess of Hereford, and Johanne his wife, have made their humble suit and petition unto us that it might please us to licence and permit them to occupy a tavern and sell wines by retail as they used to do before making of the said statute, for that they should be otherwise compelled to put away their apprentices, journeymen, and other their servants, and to break up their household to their utter undoing, having fifteen children, and none other trade or living but only by retailing of wines, wherein they had been brought up most of their lifetime:

We therefore, minding that our said subjects should be relieved in these particulars, are pleased and content, and by these presents of our special grace and certain knowledge, moreover do give licence and liberty, and do grant for us, our heirs and successors, to John Kerry and Johanne his wife, that they during their lives and the longest liver of either of them shall and may keep a tavern and sell and utter by retail any kind of wine to be drunk or spent in his or their mansion house or other place in their occupation within the city of Hereford, in such manner and form as they might have done before the making of the said statute, without any manner of loss, pain, forfeiture, imprisonment, or penalty to be by them sustained for the same. And further our will and pleasure is that the said John Kerry and Johanne his wife shall in future hereof take, have, and enjoy the full effect, benefit and advantage of this license and grant, from the first day of May last past, without any danger, loss, pain, forfeiture, or imprisonment to be to him or them for the same. In witness whereof we have caused these our letters to be made patent. Witness ourselves at Farnham the 5th day of July, the fifth year of the reign. Given under our seal'.

Was it because John had been Mayor of the city three years earlier, or was Queen Mary swayed by the thought of the fifteen children, bearing in mind that her husband, Philip of Spain, had abandoned her after only fourteen months of married life? Whichever, she died shortly after granting the Kerry's their licence.

It was presumably one of these fifteen children, a Thomas Kerry who lived in Sherfield in Kent but was described as a native of Hereford, who, in 1607, founded the Kerry or Trinity Hospital for thirteen poor widows and three unmarried men. The Hospital or Almshouses was built in 1620 and re-built in 1824. Until their demolition a few years ago they occupied a plot of ground directly across Commercial Street from the **Kerry Arms**.

It may be that the inn and grounds, together with the four adjoining shops in Commercial Street, which are now part of Chadds Store, were handed over to the Governing Body of the Trinity Hospital by Thomas Kerry, for the deeds of sale of the inn and the houses throughout the eighteenth century all refer to a leasehold property with annual reserved rents of £6 10s. to be paid to the Hospital.

With the demolition of the gate and prison, the insignificant timber-framed building which had survived so long as the **Pack Horse** was not sufficiently grand to grace the principal entrance to the city and it too fell to the hammer. A new hotel was built in its place and opened in 1848 with a new licensee, Mrs. C. Gibson. She was paying a rent of £84 per year and had to advertise for trade:

'To Families, Tourists, and the Commercial and Agricultural Community generally—The **Kerry Arms Hotel** has recently been erected on the site of the **Pack Horse**, in Bye Street, one of the most open and healthy spots in the City of Hereford; its dining, drawing and bedrooms are spacious, lofty and airy—the upper stories commanding beautiful views of Aylestone Hill, and its picturesque neighbourhood; the interior has been fitted up with the utmost regard and attention to comfort and convenience.'

The **Kerry Arms** still faces 'one of the most open spots in Hereford', but the vast amount of motorised traffic that passes close to the door can hardly be said to be healthy!

Mrs. Gibson appeared to have cornered the market for two of the more popular beers when the **Kerry Arms** opened:

'BASS'S ALES AND GUINNESS'S PORTER'

'These delicious beverages, now in such high repute amongst the faculty for their nutritious and restorative properties, may be had in their primest condition of C. Gibson, the sole agent for Hereford and its surrounding neighbourhood at the **Kerry Arms Hotel** (late the **Pack Horse**) Bye Street, Hereford, where a large cargo of each has just been received direct from Burton and Dublin.

'These beverages may be had in either casks or bottles, and having been brought into general use in private families, may be also had in the smallest quantities, each being kept on draught.'

In 1848, it is likely that these beers would have been brought to Hereford along the newly-opened Gloucester to Hereford canal, rather than by road. It was presumably Mrs. Gibson who arranged for the new hotel to be lit by gas from the then privately-owned Hereford Gas Company, which had lighted the city following an Act of 1824. For all her zeal, Mrs. Gibson lasted for only a short while and was soon replaced by William Smith. In 1851 he was advertising his inn to all 'cricketers and others visiting Hereford to witness the all-England cricket match'. Was it William Smith or the Mr. Hankins who followed him, who was 'experimenting with a gas cooker' in 1853? Allowing for such potentially explosive situations, it is perhaps surprising that the hotel continued to operate successfully for many years.

Mr. Hankins followed Mrs. Gibson's advertising zeal and reminded readers of the local paper that the new building was 'situated within 600 yards of the proposed Gloucester Station and replete with every convenience for Travellers by Rail or otherwise'. The proposed 'Gloucester Station' was the one at Barr's Court, which was completed by 1855 at a cost of £32,000.

There followed a succession of landlords including the long-standing Thomas Hill, who is mentioned in all the Directories from 1885 until 1928, when he was under notice to quit, being on a yearly tenancy. He must have been tenant for at least 43 years!

The notice to quit was because of the proposed sale of the **Kerry Arms**, 'by direction of the Hereford Municipal Charities', the body that had taken over the responsibilities for the management of the Trinity Almshouses Charity amongst others. In the sale details the hotel is described as having:

'On the Ground floor: two smoke rooms, commercial rooms, private sitting room, kitchen (with lift to first floor), scullery and larder.

On the first floor: two sitting rooms, large dining room, small store room, three bedrooms and lavatory.

On the second floor: eight bedrooms and lavatory.'

The lack of any bathroom may well indicate that the building was in some considerable need of improvement; even the notice of sale admits that the 'property is admirably suitable for conversion into a first class tourist and commercial hotel'. There was a coach entry from Union Street with the Brewhouse on one side and stables on the other and a loft over the whole. The full extent of the property for sale at that time still included the range of four shops in Commercial Street that had first been mentioned in the 18th century.

Across Commercial Street from the **Kerry Arms**, and on the narrow strip of ground between Maylord Street and Blueschool Street, was the **Bridge Inn**. It was shown on the 1858 map of the city, but was not mentioned in the Directory for that year. However, it may have been there for some considerable time before that date for the bridge referred to must have been the one by which Bye Street crossed the city ditch before the stream which flowed along it was culverted. Later in the 19th century the property was described as two shops, so it is evident that the licence had been lost. In the 1950's and '60's this building was well-known as the Black and White Café, before it was eventually demolished to make way for the Inner Relief Road.

Just across the entrance to Maylord Street from the **Bridge** was the **Five Ways Inn** which occupied part of the corner site close to Trinity Hospital. This was a beer house and was described in the Directories from about 1890 onwards as being the premises of a beer retailer rather than being an inn. It was offered for sale in 1930 when it was described as 'Freehold Premises, recently de-licensed, and formerly known as the **Five Ways Inn**.' It had a frontage to Commercial Street of 16ft. and to Maylord Street of 52ft. Bidding started at £500, but it was eventually withdrawn. After a while the property became a butcher's shop, but like many others in that area it was eventually lost to the Relief Road.

Commercial Street also contained the **Bull's Head**, which was described in 1739 as 'a commodious large house ... in Bye Street in the city ... lately used as an Inn ... having three rooms each about 20 feet square with many lesser rooms. A very large cellar, two large passages into a spacious courtyard ...', but it is otherwise unknown. The same applies to the equally mysterious **Cap and Feather**, also described as being in Bye Street, which was sold by auction at the **Fleece Tavern** in 1797. Was there also another **Bunch of Grapes** in Bye Street, from which a William Elliot apparently moved to take over the **Butcher's Arms** in Maylord Street in 1812?

In Union Street, around the corner from Commercial Square, were the several back entries to the **Kerry Arms**, the **Coach & Horses**, and the **Crown & Sceptre**. Union Street has had a variety of names—in the 18th and early 19th centuries it was Gaol Lane, not surprisingly considering that the City Gaol was in the gate building at one end, whilst the County Gaol was where the Shire Hall now stands at the other. At a still earlier date Union Street had the more respectable name of Old School Street, whilst Speede on his 1610 map gives it simply as Olde Strete.

The south-eastern side of the street accommodated the lesser inns, of which one always seems to be remembered by older Herefordians with some affection. This was the **Angler**, which apparently stopped being the **Jolly Angler** some time in the 1840's. As the **Jolly Angler** it was for sale in 1796 when it was described as newly-built. It was then no. 25 Union Street and was opposite the end of Union Passage which still leads to Commercial Road. In 1836 it was for sale again. It then consisted of a spacious bar, kitchen, parlour, excellent dining room, three bedrooms and a long, narrow passage leading through to the inevitable brewhouse. The garden stretched back for some 134 feet and included a strip of ground which was later to become part of St. Peter's School. It was most probably bought by Mr. George Harding, for in 1839 he was offering his thanks to all 'his Friends and the Public generally for their support and encouragement ... since he entered the inn'. He mentioned the thorough repair and enlargement that had taken place and announced the inevitable 'House-warming Party' with dinner tickets 'including dessert and waiters at 5 shillings each'.

It was for sale once again in 1849, presumably after George Harding had moved across the road to the **Crown and Sceptre**, together with the two adjoining cottages, presumably those to the north. Surprisingly it is not shown as an inn on Curley's 1858 plan of the city, although it is entered in the Directory for that year with William Dutton as landlord. By that time St. Peter's Main School building had been erected and the inn was probably being extended again as later Directories describe it as nos. 24 and 25. By 1888 the grounds of the **Angler** had become oddly-shaped and included parts of the original plots of both cottages to the north, presumably to make up for ground lost to the school.

By 1891 the solitary **Angler** who used the inn must have gained some partners for subsequent Directories all refer to the hostelry as the **Anglers' Inn**. James Charles Goodman was landlord for much of the latter half of the 19th century. The **Anglers'** continued to serve thirsty customers well into the second half of the 20th century, but eventually it declined in popularity and has now been closed for several years. The building still survives as part of the Marches and can be recognised from many old photographs.

At the same time as Gaol Street became Union Street, the new City Gaol was being built in what was then known as Grope Lane.

This narrow street ran from Union Street in a long curve to end up in St. Owen Street just within the site of the gate. The confusing changes of name were complete when Grope Lane became Gaol Street, and as Gaol Street it has remained although the Gaol, now the Magistrates Court, was closed in 1877. For many years the entry into Gaol Street from Union Street was very narrow because on the northern side there was the **White Horse Inn**.

This half-timbered building, then number 32 Union Street, was described as being of early 17th century date by the Royal Commission on Historic Monuments following their visit in 1928. However, the large square panelling and the curved braces would suggest an earlier date. According to an earlier writer, this building was the home of Thomas Gomond in the mid-18th century. This was apparently the Thomas Gomond who was Mayor of the city in 1777. The same writer states that it became an inn in 1816 when it was known as the **Saint Catherine Wheel**. There was another inn in the immediate area which was also called the **Catherine Wheel**. This was in the adjoining St. Peter's Square, hard against the church and is described in the next chapter. The St. Peter's Square inn was demolished shortly before 1816, so the name may well have been transferred to the Gomond House. Even so, the name did not last for long and by 1845 the inn had become the **White Horse** and is so shown on the 1858 map.

The **White Horse Hotel** advertised on its large roof board that it was associated with Wintles Brewery Ltd. of Mitcheldean who produced Health Ales and Stout. A plan of the building that was made in 1931 shows that it was surprisingly large with three bars and a smoke room on the ground floor, four bedrooms and a sitting room on the first floor, and two main bedrooms and three attic bedrooms on the second floor. It continued in use as an inn until 1937 when the owners surrendered the licence in order to open the **Broad Leys**, built to serve the new housing estates off the Ross Road. The building was used by the military during the Second World War and was demolished shortly afterwards in order to widen Gaol Street.

The building suddenly exposed by the demolition of the **White Horse** was no. 31 Union Street and old deeds indicate that in 1766 this was the **Star and Garter**. At a later date there was an inn of the same name in Commercial Road. On the opposite side of Gaol Street to the White Horse site is an inn which, until recently, was called the **New Harp**. As Hereford is so close to Wales, this could have been a Welsh Harp rather than the more usual Irish one.

Towards the end of the eighteenth century there were four building plots between Gaol Street and the County Gaol site (where the Shire Hall now stands). In 1788, the plot to the north of the gaol was vacant, but next to it was a tavern called the **Flower Pot** which was then occupied by a Mr. Griffiths. There were two other buildings between the **Flower Pot** and Gaol Street. There is no mention of an inn within this block of three buildings on the 1858 Curley plan or in the Directory for that year, but by 1862 there was an inn called the **Union** with Charles Field as landlord, which was at no. 34 Union Street.

By 1876 the **Union** had been re-named the **New Harp** and this inn is shown on the 1886 Ordnance Survey map as being the middle building of the three. It is evident that the corner building shown on the 1886 map was number 33 Union Street; the entry in the Directory for 1891 for the occupant of the house with that number and in that position is given as Mrs. Harriet Carpenter, a dress maker. In the early years of the present century the front part of Mrs. Carpenter's house was included within the **New Harp** by the simple expedient of knocking a couple of doorways through the wall which separated the two properties. The public entrance on the right led directly into the inn, whilst the doorway on the left led into what was known as 'The Cottage', a private house at the rear with a single room on each floor.

By 1926, the whole building belonged to the Stroud Brewery and they proposed a comprehensive reconstruction. The plans show that some walls and one chimney stack were re-used, but in effect a new **New Harp** arose on the corner site. With its stone-faced ground floor and half-timbering above, this is typical example of vernacular revivalism although a little later in date than the other excellent example, the **Imperial** in Widemarsh Street.

It could be suggested that the changes in name from the **Flower Pot** to the **Union** and then to the **New Harp** would have been enough for the customers of any one inn to bear, but the last few years have seen yet another change. This historic inn now suffers from a totally inappropriate name that has no connection with Hereford whatsoever—the **Oliver Twist**.

CHAPTER TEN

THE ST. OWEN STREET AREA

The eastern extremity of the market place designed by William fitzOsbern to grace his new Norman town of Hereford is where St. Owen Street gradually widens to become St. Peter's Square. Before the end of the 11th century the market place had suffered a radical change. FitzOsbern had died and, after 1075, Walter de Lacy took a leading part in the development of Hereford. Deeply religious, he arranged for a new monastic church, St. Peter's, to be built in the eastern part of the grand market place. The church was just about complete when de Lacy tragically fell from the top of the tower whilst inspecting the works.

St. Peter's became a simple parish church after its monastic functions had been combined with those of St. Guthlac's following the battles in Hereford associated with the contested succession to the throne in 1138-40. St. Guthlac's had been within the castle bailey on Castle Green, but following these events a new site was found in Commercial Road where the bus station and hospital now stand. As time went by, the space in front of St. Peter's Church gradually took on the appearance of a small and rather pleasant square.

Throughout most of its history St. Peter's Square was strategically placed to take advantage of marketing opportunities, with St. Owen Street leading out to the east and St. Peter's Street joining it to High Town. During the 18th century, and probably for many years before, there were several buildings which were attached to the eastern side of St. Peter's Church. It was between these buildings and the County Gaol that the narrow Union Street led to the great Bye Street Gate. On the other side of the square the even

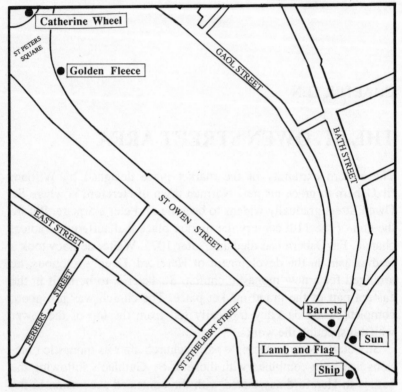

narrower Offa Street led into the old town. This was little more than a pedestrian passage until it was widened in 1957 when the Trustee Savings Bank was built on the corner.

By the end of the 18th century most of the buildings which now surround the square had already been built, but there was one notable exception. The Shire Hall, built to the design of Mr. (later Sir) Robert Smirke who went on to design the British Museum, was not completed until 1817. Before that time, this large site on the eastern side of the square contained the County Gaol.

One of the buildings attached to eastern side of St. Peter's Church was an inn, the **Catherine Wheel** briefly mentioned in the last chapter. It was described in 1790 as 'a good accustomed inn, fronting St. Owen Street and continuous to St. Peter's Church ... of a yearly value of £20.' In the sale description of 1803 the inn included stabling for 50 horses, good cellaring and a Brewhouse.

It was outside the **Catherine Wheel** that public executions were held. It is recorded of one in the latter part of the eighteenth century that, while their father was being made ready to be 'pushed off', his children were amongst the crowd collecting coppers. News of this was taken to the Court of Sessions, which was meeting at the **Mitre** in Broad Street. They gave orders for the children to be taken out of their father's sight so that he 'could swing in the air.'

One of the last of the public hangings to take place in the square was that of William Jones (alias Watkins) and Susannah Rugg in 1790. Jones was a native of Clodock and the pair had conspired together to poison Jones's wife at Longtown by the use of arsenic. A later report goes on to say: 'They were executed in St. Owen's Street ... opposite to where the old County Gaol stood. The body of Jones was taken and hung in chains at Longtown Green, near to his former residence and to where the deed was committed.' These public spectacles would doubtless have ensured that the **Catherine Wheel** was well patronised. The view of the event from the upper windows would have been particularly good! The **Catherine Wheel** was demolished at the same time as the County Gaol, presumably to improve the setting of the new Shire Hall.

Adjoining the Gaol on the St. Owen Street side was a house belonging to a Mr. Sylvester which was known by the **Sign of the Fleece**. In December 1787 it suffered 'a most dreadful fire' which entirely consumed the building and its contents. It would seem that it was rapidly rebuilt, for when Mr. Blackburne, a London architect, published his report on the County Gaol in 1790 he included the comment that 'an improper means of communication between the Keeper's house and an adjoining house' allowed the introduction of 'spirituous liquors' into the gaol. This illicit entry must have been from the **Fleece**, for in July 1804 it was ordered that 'the window that opened into the First Court of the Old Gaol from the **Fleece** be stopped up and notice given for that purpose.' This was not at all satisfactory to Mrs. Sylvester, presumably by then a widow, and she stood up for her rights. This was acknowledged at the next Sessions when a compromise was effected so that she was 'allowed to open the window but to sign an acknowledgement that it is done by leave of Sessions—no Liquors may be conveyed through the window to persons in the yard'. By that time most prisoners had been moved to the new gaol in Commercial Road and within a few years the new Shire Hall had been built—apparently without any means of obtaining drinks through a back window in the pub!

At some time around the beginning of the present century the **Fleece** was brightened up to become the **Golden Fleece Hotel**. It was then a very long and thin building which had a small public bar at the front and, approached by a long and narrow passage, a rather gloomy smoke room with very limited natural lighting at the rear.

The change of name didn't absolve the landlord from getting into trouble for the *Hereford Times* of the 27th March 1920 recorded the following event:

'CONSTABLES DRINK - LICENSEE HEAVILY FINED

'Two unusual charges were preferred against a Hereford licensee by the Chief Constable at the Hereford City police court on Monday.

'Thomas Bach, Licensee of the Golden Fleece Inn St. Peter's Street, was summoned for serving a constable of the Hereford City police force, whilst on duty, with spirituous liquor and also for harbouring the constable on the premises on March 17th. The name of the constable was not divulged.

'On March 17th at 9.10p.m. the chief constable noticed that the constable was not at the Town Hall where he had been detailed. Having his suspicions, he went to the Golden Fleece but did not immediately see the constable. He was about to leave again when he saw the constable standing behind the door leading to the bar, helmet in hand. He denied the glass on the bar was his, the Landlord when asked for an explanation said he did not think it an offence for the constable to be there, but did not suggest he did not know the constable was on duty.

'When the chief constable left the premises the licensee followed and told him he had held a licence for a number of years without complaint, that he had supplied the constable only one drink and that he would give a donation to any charitable institution if the chief constable would overlook it.

'The defendant said he had been the licensee at the Golden Fleece since 1916, and prior to that had held licences in Cheltenham and Middlesbrough for about 30 years. He said he had never been charged with any licensing offence before and produced a testimonial from the chief constable of Middlesbrough.

'The Mayor said they were satisfied on the evidence that the policeman was on duty and that the Defendant knew he was on duty. They convicted the licensee in both cases and find him £5 for each, with 3 guineas costs.'

The Inn was owned by the Stroud Brewery and Thomas Bach continued as landlord for at least another decade, apparently not getting into trouble with the law again. The **Golden Fleece** survived the closure of the Shire Hall as the County Council headquarters, following the unpopular creation of the County of Hereford & Worcester. It also survived the construction of the collection of islands and bus stops which still disfigure St. Peter's Square and makes such a poor setting for the war memorial and church. The two small drinking rooms and the narrow passage which led through the building to the rear yard have all been amalgamated into one large room, but the thinness of the plot—doubtless one of those laid out by William fitzOsbern for his French settlers over 900 years ago—is still apparent.

St. Owen Street, with its predominantly Georgian buildings, has been mainly residential for many years and is not a place to find inns and hotels. However, as with all the other roads leading into Hereford, hostelries tended to exist close to the city gates and the area around St. Owen's Gate was no exception. The city wall still approaches the street from each side—on the south it is the visible side wall of what was, until recently, Townsend's Stationery Supplies; on the north it forms the boundary between the **Barrels** and a restaurant called the Taste of Raj. Indeed, the stone-built section of the latter was doubtless a part of the porter's lodge that faced into the narrow Gaol Street. This street was the back lane that acted as a service road for all the large properties on the north side of St. Owen Street. St. Owen's Gate, which joined the two stretches of wall, was demolished in 1786 and the ditch was probably culverted at the same time.

Previous to 1967 the narrow road which still runs along the out-of-town side of the **Barrels** was the southern end of Bath Street. The arrangement of the streets in this area was altered when an extension to Bath Street was made as part of the Inner Relief Road. This extension cut across what had previously been St. Owen's burial ground, and the earlier line of Bath Street was cut off and renamed Harrison Street.

There are several inns which were associated with the Gate—the **Barrels**, built partly on top of the ditch which originally ran on the outside of the city wall and the **Sun**, on the opposite side of what was until recently Bath Street. Both survive to the present day, but others have been lost. There was the **Lamb and Flag Tavern** which was on the opposite side of St. Owen Street to the **Barrels**, facing the entry to Gaol Street. This inn had been built against the inside face of the city wall and was apparently quite large, being the equivalent of three of the present properties. It may well be that the **Barrels**, which until recently was called the **Lamb Inn**, was a successor to the **Lamb and Flag**.

The present **Lamb** would have been built shortly after St. Owen's Gate had been taken down and is first mentioned in 1800. In 1848, George Russell, who had occupied the inn for ten years, advertised 'All that old-established and well-accustomed Inn and Premises called the **Lamb Inn**, with Malthouse, extensive stabling, lock-up yard, and every other requisite convenience for carrying out an extensive business, and to which a good Country as well as Counter Trade is attached.'

The property was for sale in 1906, but subject to a twenty-one year lease (from August 1896) to Ind Coope & Co. Mr. J.B. Barling held the Hotel as a yearly tenant of Ind Coope, but they retained the yard and stables as their local depot.

The **Lamb** became the **Barrels** in 1987, and is now the home of the Wye Valley Brewery. At one time almost every inn had its own brewery—now it is a rare but very welcome sight.

A late 18th century sketch showing St. Owen's Gate and a building with an inn sign, probably that of the Sun

The **Sun**, on the opposite side of the narrow Bath Street, was built close to the stone bridge by which traffic along St. Owen Street crossed the city ditch. The sketch of the gate, opposite, which appears to have been drawn from the outside as there are traces of a bridge, and which must date earlier than 1786, shows a large building, with a hanging sign appropriate to an inn, in the position of the **Sun** Inn. The present building is of late 18th or early 19th century date. It was certainly an inn in 1832, for during that year the landlord, one W. Phillips, attempted to change the name to the **Angel**. He was unsuccessful and since then it has continued as the **Sun**, resisting change whenever possible. In recent years it was well-known, to its regulars and with certain visitors to the city, for

the wooden barrels of Bulmers cider which stood on the bar counter, tapped and ready to serve. Woe betide the unwary drinker who thought that this easy-to-drink apple juice would have little effect.

There was another inn that was associated with St. Owen's Gate—the **Ship**—on the corner of St. Owen Street and Mill Street. The city wall, leaving St. Owen's Gate in a southerly direction, turns at right angles, and forms the boundary between the properties facing St. Owen Street and those in Cantilupe Street. The abrupt change in direction was at the point where the thirteenth century defences met up with the Saxon defences built some 300 years earlier. From this point the old defensive line was reused following a gradual curve to the north-east corner of Castle Green, the bailey of Hereford Castle. The **Ship Inn** was on this bend and would thus have had the city ditch running through its yard and the city wall as its rear boundary.

The **Ship** may have been on that site for a considerable length of time in one form or another. Although it would have interfered with the defensive potential of the wall and ditch, it was directly opposite the site on which St. Owen's church had been built. This was one of the two churches that was damaged during the Civil War siege and demolished therefafer. Had there been a **Ship** inn there before the Civil War, it is almost certain that it would have suffered the same fate as the church, but could well have been re-built.

The inn was held on a lease by the Hereford Brewery for a term of 14 years from February 1890 at a rent of £70 rising to £75. It was described in the 1898 sale as comprising 'Brewhouse, Premises and Cottage adjoining'. It managed to survive into the 20th century, but finally closed its doors in 1913. The site is now occupied by the St. Owen's Court flats.

There are a few other inns mentioned in old documents as being in St. Owen Street. The earliest would appear to be yet another **Catherine Wheel** which was in the vicinity of the gate in 1436 and belonged to St. Guthlac's Priory. It ceased to be an inn in 1459. Another early one is **Wilton's Ynne**, mentioned in 1517 as the town house of Grey de Wilton of Wilton Castle, Ross. Then there was the **Hand & Shears**, noted as being in St. Owen Street in 1796, and the **Three Stirrups**, somewhere in St. Owen's parish in 1737. A mysterious **Talbot**, which is also described as being in St. Owen's in 1805, still remains unidentified, and somewhere there was one of the several inns which was called the **Prince of Wales**. Finally there was the **Boars Head Tavern**, which was home to the Boar's Head Society, one of the many friendly societies in the city, in 1794. The landlord at that time must have suffered somewhat from his name—he was Mr. Bull!

In this chapter an attempt has been made to put St. Owen's Gate into context with the inns that grew up around it. The same must have been the case with all the gates, but much visible evidence was lost when the Inner Relief Road was built in the late 1960's.

CHAPTER ELEVEN

LOST TO THE RING ROAD

It is becoming difficult for many people to remember back to the time when Hereford did not have the Inner Relief Road, as the present ring road is more properly called. The choice between an inner relief road and one which bypassed Hereford completely was debated furiously for many years and it was only the personal intervention of the then Minister for Transport that resolved the problem. The intention was to build a new four-lane bridge across the river a little upstream of the historic Wye bridge and connect this to a series of widened roads that would encircle the city following the line of the city ditch. It was appreciated that the widening of these roads would involve the loss of a considerable number of buildings including several inns.

From the new bridge, a road was built to connect with the southern end of Victoria Street which had previously finished at the Barton Road—St. Nicholas Street junction. Victoria Street was then widened on the east exposing the city wall for the first time for many years. The crossing of Eign Street required much demolition, for the new road, as it approached the roundabout to the north, included not just Edgar Street, but also the western part of Wall Street and the buildings between the two. This stretch of the new road actually cut across the line of the city wall. The reconstructed wall around the Tesco superstore preserves the feeling of a walled town, but is well inside the actual line of the medieval wall.

Along Newmarket Street, the buildings on the south side, which had been constructed against the city wall, were all demolished exposing the remains of the city wall along this section. On the far side of Widemarsh Street, the historic gatehouse building—now the Farmers Club—was saved at the expense of the buildings to the north. The trail of destruction continued along Blueschool Street with demolition first on the north and then, as the new road curved to the south to incorporate the eastern part of Maylord Street, a further section of the medieval wall line was lost. The crossing of Commercial Square—previously a roundabout—involved some demolition on the city side to avoid the then newly-built Franklin Barnes building on the north-east corner. Bath Street was only widened significantly near Commercial Square, but the line was totally altered where it joined into St. Owen Street. At this point a new road was built across the old St. Owen's burial ground and the old line of Bath Street was sealed off behind a car park and re-named Harrison Street.

Bath Street, Blueschool Street, Newmarket Street and Victoria Street were all roads which had gradually developed on the outside of the city ditch. They appear on Taylor's map, produced in the middle of the eighteenth century, as rather pleasant tree-lined walks rather than proper roads. During the 19th century they gradually became built up as yards, shops and houses were constructed along their lengths. As we follow the line of the Inner Relief Road, it is only in areas adjacent to the city gates that any historic pubs are likely to be found.

In the previous chapter the inns which were associated with the St. Owen's Gate area were described. Because the new road was built across the disued St. Owen's burial ground, none of these inns were demolished. There was only one inn in Bath Street. This was the short-lived **Bakers Arms**, a beer-house near the junction with Commercial Road, which was mentioned in 1876. A typical inn sign would recall the former close connection between bakers and brewers; indeed, in the late medieval period both trades were often practised by the same man. The **Bakers Arms** was yet another inn where the licence was extinguished and compensation paid to those affected. In this case, the compensation was fixed by the Inland Revenue at £750, somewhat less than the £1,150 that the owners had asked for. It was split as £683 6s. 8d. for the owners and £66 13s. 4d. for the licensee. The beerhouse closed in May 1916.

Where the Relief Road crossed Commercial Square, the **Kerry Arms**, standing on the city side, was saved, but in Commercial Street the buildings on both sides of the entrance to Maylord Street were demolished and that section of Maylord Street was incorporated into the dual carriageway. The demolition included the buildings which had at an earlier date housed the **Five Ways** and the **Bridge**, both short-lived pubs of the late 19th and early 20th centuries which were closed well before the Relief Road was proposed and have already been described in chapter nine.

There were two inns in Blueschool Street in the early years of the present century. These were the attractively-named **Railway Bell** and the more prosaic **Vine**. The **Railway Bell**, often simply called the **Bell**, had its back to the city wall about half-way between Commercial Square and the junction with Widemarsh Street, adjoining the narrow Blueschool or Bell Passage. The front was set back a little way from the street because it had originally been built on the narrow strip of ground between the city wall and the ditch. The latter had eventually been culverted between the pub and Blueschool Street, but the area was obviously not really fit to build on. Even so, the bar, a miniature little room which protruded out in front of the building, must have been built almost entirely on this reclaimed land. It was balanced at the other end of the building with a W.C. that doubtless made use of the culverted ditch for the removal of effluent. The porch, next to the bar, led into the smoke room, a small kitchen and a ground-level cellar. The remainder of the ground floor consisted of two sets of three stables. Because of its situation, the building was only one room thick, the rear wall being part of the city wall. There were three doorways which led through this stone wall into a narrow yard containing a lean-to shed and what appears to have been an essential feature of all pubs 100 or so years ago, the dung pit!

The **Railway Bell** was certainly functioning in the late 1850's but, bearing in mind its name and the late arrival of the railway in Hereford, probably not much earlier. It was eventually closed in 1909 when the annual renewal of the licence was refused. The inn site is now underneath the Inner Relief Road, but the blocked doorways which once led from the kitchen and stables to the rear yard can still be traced in the stretch of city wall which runs between the

Relief Road and the 'bus lay-by on the northern side of the Maylord Orchards development.

The **Vine** was on the opposite side of Blueschool Street to the **Railway Bell**, a little nearer to the Widemarsh Street junction. There was already a **Vine Tree Tavern** in 1826, but the building which is shown on the 1886 Ordnance Survey plan was probably built during the third quarter of the 19th century. The details of the sale in 1898 give a good impression of a public house of this type:

'Well situated in Blueschool Street, in the City of Hereford and on one of the main routes from the Railway Station to the Cattle and Produce Markets and in close proximity thereto.

'Brick built and slated, it contains:

'On the Ground Floor: Large well-fitted bar, private parlour, kitchen and scullery adjoining, large store place, brick-paved and drained, with side door to private parlour. Opening from the street is a large yard, paved and drained, at the side of the house, with a flap to extensive cellarage.

'On the First Floor: is a good sized sitting room, bedroom, and two larger ditto divided by a partition, the removal of which would convert them into a good club room.

'On the Top Floor: Two good bedrooms, each with a fireplace, and one with large cupboard adjoining.'

There was an additional advantage to any potential purchaser, for included in the sale details was a note that 'With the foregoing is included a shed or booth on Hereford Racecourse known as No. 4 Booth'. These Booths were apparently of some importance and were sometimes sold separately. One, sold by auction at the **New Inn** on the 6th April 1841 was described as: 'All that substantial, roomy, and newly-erected Booth, or Tavern, situate on the Racecourse, at Widemarsh, being the nearest to the Gold Stand and commanding the best view of the course and long length.'

Although the **Vine** was very much a back street inn, it seems only to have been successful with female licensees. Mrs. Lizzie Andrews saw it through the turn of the century and was followed by Mrs. Elizabeth Davies. It was not long after Cecil Wheatstone took over in the late 1920's that there was a fire which 'originated in an ash pit beneath the grate, the existence of which was unknown'. The fire was sufficiently serious to be recorded in the *Hereford Times* in December 1930. Mr. Wheatstone did not last long, and by 1935 Mrs. E. Palamountain was behind the bar, to be followed in a short while by Mrs. Mabel Moore. By 1941 Thomas Jordan had taken over—he was presumably responsible for the closure of the inn for he is recorded at the same address in 1951 but without any mention of it being a public house. The building survived until 1966. Although the **Vine**, or **Vine Tree** as it was occasionally known, was closed well before the Relief Road was built, it was very much a victim of the general blight which had encompassed the whole of this area for well over a quarter of a century as the various proposals for improving the flow of traffic in Hereford were considered.

The **Victoria Hotel** was an imposing corner building on the west side of Widemarsh Street and the northern side of Newmarket Street. It was very much a product of the mid 19th century and was originally called the **Mazeppa** after the coach which, in 1837, set up the record-breaking time of fifteen hours for the journey from Hereford to London. Dunkling and Wright in their book *Pub Names of Britain* have a more entertaining story for this early name. Apparently Lord Byron published a poem in 1819 which concerned a Polish nobleman called Ivan Stepanovitch Mazeppa. This unfortunate young man was discovered in embarrassing circumstances

Widemarsh Street looking towards the city centre before the Inner Relief Road was built. The Victoria Hotel is on the right, with the Wellington on the far corner

with the wife of a local magnate. His punishment was to be bound naked to the back of a horse which was then lashed furiously. The horse galloped off and did not stop until it died. Mazeppa, according to the poem, was rescued by peasants and lived to tell the tale. It would seem that the reputation of Mazeppa for travelling fast was first transferred to the coach and then to the inn!

As the **Victoria Hotel**, this inn is included in the Directories from 1885 onwards. It belonged to the Stroud Brewery and had at least one major face-lift, if not a complete rebuild, during its relatively short life. The 19th century corner building was mainly single-storey, but with a small three-storey block on the Widemarsh Street frontage that contained just two bedrooms on the first floor and one on the second. This relatively small hotel was replaced with a much grander building around 1923, although some of the inner parts of the earlier building survived. Within a year or so a club room had been added on the first floor on the Newmarket Street side. It closed on the 7th October 1967 and was then demolished to make way for the Relief Road.

The **Wellington** which is on the opposite corner of Newmarket Street, has been described in chapter eight. This inn, which was re-built as a result of an earlier street widening, was saved at the expense of the **Victoria**. The **Cattle Market Tavern** was also much more fortunate than its nearby neighbour. It was saved from demolition because it was set back a little way from Newmarket Street. This inn, which is still open, is described in chapter thirteen.

It is now difficult to appreciate that Newmarket Street probably started its life as a pleasant country lane following the outside of the city ditch, then filled with running water from the Yazor Brook, from Widemarsh Gate in a gentle curve around to Eign Gate. There was an alternative route which followed Bowsey Lane, as Wall Street was then called, along the inside of the city wall from the one gate to the other. The ground to the north of Newmarket Street was part of the area of the city which was called the Portfields in the 18th century and before. It was eventually purchased by the City Council for use as the New Cattle Market. The **Cattle Market Tavern** was then ideally placed for use by thirsty farmers and their stockmen, but competition was bound to grow along Newmarket Street.

The only space which was left for development was the narrow strip of ground between the city wall and the ditch and this was gradually colonised with the new buildings making use of the city wall as their own rear wall. These buildings faced onto Newmarket Street and, in the mid-19th century, were still approached by a series of small bridges across the ditch. As pressure for additional space grew, the ditch was made narrower and narrower until it was eventually culverted and the buildings could then extend right up to the Newmarket Street frontage.

One of these buildings was the **Globe**, which was half way along Newmarket Street. It was opened a little before 1872, possibly shortly after the **Globe** in Broad Street closed, and by 1890 it belonged to Charles Watkins and Sons. They had sold it well before the grand Hereford Brewery sale in 1898 for it was not included in the catalogue. In 1910, it was for sale again as the owner, Mr. Bennett, was about to go abroad. Although small, the **Globe** had a bar, bar-parlour, smoke room and private smoke room, with a Jug and Bottle in the hall. Not surprisingly, it completely filled the 32 feet square plot with no room whatsoever for a yard. In the late 1920's Albert Footitt moved to the **Globe** from the **Whalebone**, but must not have been very successful for the inn closed on the 30th September 1932 and by 1935 the building had become the new home for the up-and-coming firm of auctioneers, F. H. Sunderland & Co.

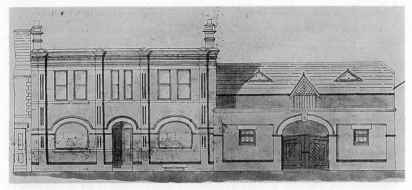

The Newmarket Street elevation of the Wheatsheaf as proposed and built in 1901

A few doors along Newmarket Street from the **Globe** at no. 17, was the **Wheatsheaf** at no. 22. Not surprisingly, considering its position close to the rear access, the inn and the adjoining house, no. 23, both belonged to the Hereford Brewery. At the Brewery sale, the inn was let to Mrs. Eliza Davies for £24 10s. per annum, but the house was let to Harry Cole, a Clerk at the Brewery 'at the inadequate rental of £12 per annum'. At that time both were set well back from Newmarket Street with yards in front. The Hereford & Tredegar Brewery took over and Harry Cole must have lost his cheap house, for in 1901 the new owners applied for permission to carry out improvements. This work included extending the inn to the edge of Newmarket Street and rebuilding the adjoining house as a yard and stable block approached from the street through rather fine double doors. The **Wheatsheaf** continued to serve the thirsty farmers from the Cattle Market across the road and the employees of Harrison & Bowen's skin and hide centre next door, until it was finally forced out of business by the plans for the Inner Relief Road.

Before the large roundabout was built, Newmarket Street curved gradually to the south, becoming one with Edgar Street as they together approached the junction with Eign Street. Until 1966, this junction was famous for possessing the only set of traffic lights in the whole county of Herefordshire. Efficiency was guaranteed at peak traffic times by switching off the lights and putting a policemen on point duty! This junction was also important to travellers and pedestrians because it had inns on three of its four corners—the **Victoria Vaults** and the **West Midland Inn** faced each other across the end of Edgar Street, whilst across Eign Street was the **Red Lion**. The fourth corner was taken over by the various enterprises of the King family: T.A. King & Co., Sculptor, Carver & Monumental Mason at the rear; the single-storey garage and motor-cycle showroom of C.F. King & Co. at the front; and next door towards the city centre, King's Radio.

The **Victoria Wine Vaults**, not to be confused with the inn with a similar name at the Newmarket Street—Widemarsh Street junction, was built in the second half of the 19th century. It started its life as the **Victoria Inn** but had been re-named the **Victoria Wine**

The Eign Street, Victoria Street and Edgar Street junction at a busy time with a policeman on point duty, looking north from Victoria Street. The Victoria Vaults is central and the Red Lion on the left

The junction of Eign Street and Victoria Street looking west before the Relief Road was built. The gabled building is the Red Lion. The buildings in the middle distance still survive

Vaults by the 1870's. As vehicular traffic increased at this busy junction, this large, three-storey, brick-built public house probably suffered from a gradual decline in its trade. Originally, it had an arched entrance in Edgar Street which led into a small yard, but towards the end of its life, this entrance was sealed off and converted to become a second-hand shop called Sheila's Fit Shop. Next to this blocked entry but still within the inn building, was a transport café. As this offered accommodation as well as food, it must have made use of some of the upper floors of the inn.

Along the Eign Street frontage the public house building also included a shop which sold musical instruments. The inn and its shops occupied the whole of the corner site and was surrounded by a branch of Jessons—The Working Man's Stores—which had a shop in Edgar Street and a store in Eign Street. Jessons also occupied the old **Maidenhead** on the opposite side of Eign Street and closer to the city centre, where they still have a shop. The 'Wine' was officially removed from the name of the inn in 1934, but the **Victoria Vaults** continued to serve customers until it was demolished early in 1968.

The **West Midland Inn** on the northern side of Eign Street had a more restricted corner site being part of the block of buildings between Edgar Street and Wall Street. It was built in the second half of the 19th century, but did not have a long life as a public house although it was often used by the mechanics working at King's Garage who would be treated to drinks by delighted owners after their cherished motor vehicles had been successfully repaired. However, the licence was not renewed in 1907 and shortly afterwards it had been opened as a grocery store belonging to John H. Dean. As Dean's Stores it was known to several generations of Herefordians until it finally closed and the windows were boarded up in the 1960's.

The **Red Lion** had a much longer history than the other two corner pubs but, although the building survived the construction of the Inner Relief Road, the new road had effectively cut it off from the centre of the city and much of its trade was inevitably lost. It continued to serve a decreasing number of customers for another ten years, but the site had little attraction as a public house and it was finally demolished in 1978 to make way for a development of 22 flats.

Although the building has disappeared, the **Red Lion** has a long and distinguished history as the principal inn on the main approach road to the city from Wales. It was mentioned in 1661, when the inhabitants of Eign Ward were fined for not maintaining in a fit condition the nearby pump, but its origins probably go back much further.

The inn was for sale in October 1841, when the tenant landlord was William Tranter. Apart from the inn, there was 'the Brewhouse, Lock-up Coach House, Saddle Room, and Stabling (for 38 horses)'. At that time the building was described as being 'in a thorough state of repair and offering capabilities for carrying on both a Town and Country business of great magnitude, being a very old-established House, and in one of the best situations in the city'. William Tranter left in 1842 and his place was taken by Thomas Williams, who moved from the **Ox** in White Cross Street.

The old **Red Lion** was a multi-gabled, timber-framed building which was described in 1906 as 'an historic landmark' that 'might well have figured in the pages of the novelists of the early Victorian era. Smoke Rooms less than 6 feet high, with beams in the ceilings, no two rooms on a floor of the same level, a rabbit-warren of bedrooms, and rooms where the beds lay on the floor because there was no room for them in the ordinary position'. By this time its great yard, in full use every market day, could accommodate nearly a couple of hundred horses and, should their owners imbibe too much during the day, they could have the beds on the floor or even rent a section of rail in one of the outhouses and sleep standing-up!

The **Red Lion** belonged to the Stroud Brewery Company, and its success led to them producing plans for a replacement fourteen-bedroom hotel. They argued that the foundations had given way on the side of the Old Eign Brook and that repair was impossible. This was a reference to the stream that, until the middle of the 18th century, had run down the centre of Eign Street on its way to feed the city ditch. The plans were approved at the Annual Licensing Meeting in February 1908 and shortly afterwards the historic building was demolished to be replaced with a three-storey stone building which, although it included some exposed timber framing on the upper floor, had relatively little character. The following year an extensive range of stabling was built in the inn yard, which then extended southwards as far as Cross Street.

The inn continued with relatively few problems although in October 1930, the landlord, Jack Gordon Hodges, was caught

The Victoria Street elevation for the new Red Lion as proposed by the architect

serving drinks after midnight. He said, in mitigation, that they were friends and 'I think I should consider myself lacking in hospitality if I did not have at any rate a cup of cocoa for them'. Mr. Hodges was quoted as saying to the police that he would ensure that they were in the hotel register by morning and asked them to tear up their report and forget everything. They didn't, and he was fined £1 for each person found in the pub plus a guinea costs.

Victoria Street is now a busy dual-carriageway leading directly to the Greyfriars Bridge across the Wye. There used to be a series of yards and sheds on the eastern side, such as Holloway & Webb's Camping Shop, which backed up against and completely concealed the City Wall. At the southern end of the street, before the bridge was built, most of the traffic turned left into St. Nicholas Street on the way to cross the river by the old Wye Bridge. A few cars turned right into the short White Friars Street and from there into Barton Road. Ahead, and visible from along the whole length of Victoria Street, was the **Barton Tavern**. Rather small, but three stories high and oddly-shaped because of its angled corner site, it even had two addresses; the front door being 11 St. Nicholas Street and the side door no. 1 White Friars Street. It probably became an inn or tavern in the latter half of the 19th century and around the turn of the century was functioning well in the hands of Steven Herbert who advertised his home-brewed beer on specially minted tokens.

It was offered for sale in 1930 following the death of the land-lady, Mrs. Sarah Elizabeth Beeks. At that time it contained 'Bar, Smoke room, Sitting room, four good-sized bedrooms, Kitchen with modern range, Scullery, Wash-house and a W.C.' At the rear was a 'small yard with the usual sanitary accommodation' and beneath 'excellent stone-built cellarage extending underneath the adjoining premises, with entries in the house and from St. Nicholas Street'. The large cellar could suggest that at one time there had been an inn with some pretensions on this site just outside the medieval Friars' Gate.

The auction was on April 30th at the Law Society's Rooms in East Street. An opening bid of £2,500 was made but the property was withdrawn at £3,000. It was sold a little while later to the Alton Court Brewery Co. of Ross for an undisclosed sum. The **Barton Tavern** continued to serve customers until the compulsory purchase order was made. It closed in 1964, one of the first inns to suffer for the new Relief Road, as it was in the way of the approach to the new bridge. The site of this inn is now underneath the western carriageway of the Relief Road, right in the middle of the junction with Barton Road.

CHAPTER TWELVE

LEADING TO WALES

There are two roads which leave the centre of the city in a westerly direction leading towards Wales. The main one is Eign Street, which for several hundred years led from fitzOsbern's great market through the historic Eign Gate to the Above Eign suburb. The Yazor Brook flowed towards the city from the north-west, creating a series of pools in the middle of the main road for several hundred yards on its way to feed the city ditch. Just before the gate it was joined from the north by the Eign Brook, and when the joint streams arrived at the gate, one branch went north and then east to encircle the walled city and eventually feed the moat around Hereford Castle, whilst the other branch led directly south to flow into the Wye a little way above the old Bridge.

The secondary road leading into the city was closer to the river. It left the walled city through the relatively minor Friars' Gate and from there led into Barton Lane. This had been the main western gateway of the Saxon town and before the Norman Conquest would have been well used. It lost much of its importance when the Norman town with its new approach roads was built to the north and even more when the defensive line was extended to include the new town.

The **Barton Tavern**, described in the previous chapter, was one of the two inns just outside the Friars' Gate, the other one being a short distance further out along Barton Road, on the northern side. This was the **Royal Oak**, which opened in the 1870's, about the same time that the inn of the same name in Bridge Street was closed. The new **Royal Oak** even took the old inn sign from its

The Royal Oak

namesake! There is no indication that there was ever an inn here before the 1870's so this one may well have opened in response to the success of the Newport to Hereford railway which had opened to Barton Station in 1854. It was unfortunate for the **Royal Oak** that the station, which was just around the corner from the inn, was closed to passenger traffic in 1893. This followed an agreement which allowed the Midland Railway to use Barr's Court station on the other side of the city. All was not lost, for Barton continued to be used for freight traffic until as recently as 1979 although the line to the south, which crossed the river at Hunderton Bridge, had been closed since 1967. Throughout its life, the **Royal Oak** must have reaped some benefit from the railway, for it too closed its doors shortly after the Barton depot finally closed.

Continuing out along Barton Road, past the entry to Station Road (now a cul-de-sac) and across the road is an inn called the **Antelope**. Names such as this seem to be designed to confuse the innocent historian for it is not immediately obvious that this public house was until recently called the **Railway Inn**. It is over a quarter of a century since the last train passed under the adjoining Barton Road bridge and shook the inn to its foundations, so it is perhaps reasonable for it to have taken a new identity.

When it was opened, this house was called the **Barton Railway Inn**, but the Barton was dropped from the sign in 1899 shortly after the station had closed to passenger traffic. Inns such as this, positioned deliberately close to the station, would have anticipated a reasonable amount of custom from travellers using the railway. However, Barton Station was sufficently large and busy to have had its own licensed Refreshment Rooms. Following the closure of the station to pasengers, this licence was allowed to lapse in September 1893.

The change of name to the **Antelope** took place in 1978. The Royal Navy has had ships called the Antelope since at least the sixteenth century. The last in line was a frigate adopted by the city and which took part in the Falklands conflict where it was sunk by Argentinian aircraft in May, 1982. When the inn name was changed, the new sign was unveiled by the then commanding officer of the ship.

The excellent map of Hereford produced by Timothy Curley in 1858 as a base for the new sewerage scheme, provides many details about the development of the city and occasionally produces an extra morsel of information about Hereford pubs. This is the case with Friar Street which runs parallel to Victoria Street and joins Barton Road to Eign Street. In 1858, the western side of the street, then called Quakers Lane, had only just started to be developed. To the north there was the new Scudamore School, set well back from the street, whilst further south there was the Iron and Brass Foundry that had been built by Captain Redford in 1834.

On the other side of the street, the new St. Nicholas' Church was about to be built on the corner with Barton Road. To the north of the church site were several terraces of small houses with short gardens, some backing onto the disused St. Nicholas' burial ground and others adjoining gardens of similar properties in Victoria Street. Half way along the longest terrace and almost opposite the entrance to Radford's Foundry, Curley marks one house, which backed onto the burial ground, as the **Old Bear**.

Virtually nothing is known about this drinking house, which in its heyday must have been mainly patronised by the workers at the Foundry, for it was closed well before the end of the 19th century. Could this have been the house of ill-repute in Quakers Lane that the ill-fated Walter Carwardine was said to have visited after he had conducted his business at the Assizes in April 1831? Early in the evening he had been drinking in the **Red Lion**, on the corner of Eign Street and Victoria Street, where he had been involved in a drunken row. From there he went round the corner into Quakers Lane to visit the brothel. His body was found the following morning in a pool at the end of Quakers Lane, presumably where the Yazor Brook ran down the middle of Eign Street. This was one of the many incidents of violence that occurred in Hereford in the early years of the 19th century, before the city police was formed. Although three men were soon convicted of the murder, this crime attracted much public concern. There was a general feeling that the streets of the city were no longer safe at night and because of this the ratepayers successfully petitioned the mayor to establish a more efficient policing system.

In Eign Street and almost opposite to the entry to Friars Street, Curley shows yet another pub, the **Union**. This is once again the only mention of what must have been a short-lived inn. It was set well back from the road, separated from the carriageway by the Yazor Brook which was still open at the time. Next to it on the city side, but protruding further into the street, was the **Prince of Wales**. This was one of several inns in Hereford with this name. Were they all named after Queen Victoria's eldest son Edward, or did some refer to an earlier prince? One was in St. Owen Street in the early 19th century, and another was functioning in Broad Street around 1850. The multiplicity of Princes is a source of some confusion which is compounded by an advertisement that was placed in the *Hereford Journal* on the 22nd November 1842. 'To be let for an Inn, to be called the **Prince of Wales**, within half a mile of Hereford. A good, substantially built House with 10 good bedrooms, roomy cellaring and stabling, large garden etc.' Could this have been the inn in Eign Street? It is less than half a mile from the city centre and doesn't look as though it could ever have had ten bedrooms even though it was three stories high and was listed as 53 and 54 Eign Street. Perhaps the bedrooms in the **Union** were included as well!

The Eign Street **Prince of Wales** appears to have first opened in 1863 with John Graty as landlord. In 1876 Mrs. Graty, presumably

John's widow, was in charge, but by 1885 the landlord was William Thomas Graty who could well have been their son. A little while later it was taken over by Messrs. Arnold, Perrett & Co, who added an extension at the rear to provide a sitting room for the landlord. This had little effect on the rather poor trade and the inn closed in 1914, to reopen as a furniture shop the following year.

The buildings which housed the **Union** and the **Prince of Wales** still survive, although the former has had a single-storey shop added to the front to bring it to the street edge. Both buildings appear to have had little maintenance in recent years and are now in rather poor condition. Across the road, in the centre of the row of shops between Friar Street and Victoria Street, a short-lived inn that was called the **Brewery** had William Cooper as landlord in 1851.

One reason for the failure of the **Brewery**, the **Union** and the **Prince of Wales** may have been the success of the **Horse and Groom**, only a few doors further along, just past the Congregational Chapel. This inn was, until recently, nos. 49 and 50 Eign Street, but this numbering gives little impression of the extremely large grounds behind the inn. The wide and long yard and garden continued back as far as the Eign Brook, but just over a hundred years ago this may not have been very pleasant for next door the equally large property was the home of the Eign Gate Tannery. The many open tan pits, which would have had an all-pervading smell, adjoined the stream and were very close to the inn garden.

This inn could be of considerable antiquity for it apparently belonged to St. Giles' Hospital which was founded in 1290. The inn was present in 1826 when the licensee William Williams entered his recognizance. Around the middle of the 19th century, William Taylor obtained a reasonably long lease on the whole establishment. After he died, his widow, Elizabeth, who was then living in Claremont Place, sub-let the inn to Charles Brown. In her will she left the remainder of the leasehold to her sister apart from an annuity of £20 per annum payable to her niece, Elizabeth Gomery. In 1858, when Charles Brown was still the landlord, the **Horse and Groom** was contributing the sum of £95 per annum in rental to the Charity Commissioners.

In 1913 additions were made to the main building including a Wash House next to the Cider House, and a bathroom complete with a 'geyser' over the bath. It still belonged to the Municipal Trustees (who managed all the Hererford charities) in 1920 when the Governors of St. Giles' Hospital signed a licence to assign the lease of the inn to a new tenant, Mr. Harry Pearman, who 'had signed an undertaking that he would not, during the continuance of the lease, cater for Char-a-Banc parties on Sundays'. Was Harry Pearman the son or grandson of the Sarah Ann Pearman who had by that time been at the Old Harp in Widemarsh Street for some 56 years?

By 1928, the Stroud Brewery Co. had taken over the **Horse and Groom** and they carried out several changes to improve efficiency. The main entrance continued to lead into a passage which went straight through the building, but the bar, on the left, was improved with wall seating, a service area, and a counter. The smoke room and club room on the right, which were behind the tap room, were joined together to make a dining room which had a new kitchen and service area adjoining. Improvements continued in 1934 following proposals for a squash court in the rear yard.

The **Horse and Groom** continues to practise its traditional role as a public house. Its yard no longer contains the many stables where visitors, riding in from the west, would have been able to leave their horses for the day. But little has really changed—many of the sons and grandsons of those turn-of-the-century travellers now leave their cars parked in the yard on market days to ensure that they do not become entangled with the complexities of the Inner Relief Road.

A little way past the **Horse and Groom** a slightly hump-backed bridge took Eign Street over the railway. On the left a road led down to Barton Station and on the right was the access to the Hay and Brecon Railway Station at Moorfields. The latter, although only catering for a small rural line, started off with its own licensed Refreshment Rooms. They were only in operation for some twelve years for in 1875 all the passenger traffic was transferred to Barton Station. The **Horse and Groom** would have continued to reap some benefit from railway passengers for another twenty years or so until Barton Station was also closed.

In the early years of this century, Eign Street became White Cross Street directly after the turning which led down to Barton

Station, and a little further on White Cross Street changed to White Cross Road after the turning for White Horse Street. This was all very confusing and White Cross Street has now become part of White Cross Road. The turning which once went down to Barton Station is now the road leading to Sainsburys supermarket.

A little way along what was White Cross Street, shortly after the railway bridge and close to the corner with Ryeland Street, was the **Cambrian Arms**. This was one of several inns that grew up in the Whitecross area of the city to serve the new housing that was being built in the second half of the 19th century. Thomas Prosser was the first landlord and was followed in the mid 1890's by John Graty, probably a member of the same family that ran the **Prince of Wales** just up the road for many years. Robert Fenton was landlord in 1917, but by 1935 the street Directory only includes Mrs. Alice Fenton, presumably his widow. She remained there for many years and was still the landlady in 1951. The inn continued to have a licence into the 1970's, but has since closed.

Leading from the north side of what was White Cross Street was Canon Moor Lane, later called Plough Street and now Plough Lane. At the corner stands the **Plough**. This is a very typical public house building of late 1930's date, but the site has a much longer history. When the Inspectors for the Royal Commission on Historic Monuments visited in the late 1920's they found a timber-framed inn which they described as having been built in the 16th century, although by the time of their visit it had been refronted in brick. They also described a timber-framed barn which stood just to the north of the house.

The **Plough** originally belonged to a charity called Price's Hospital, which had been established in the 17th century by William Price, a citizen and merchant of London. He died before the Hospital had been completed and the work was finished under the care of the Mayor and Aldermen of the city. Price's Almshouses, as the Hospital is called, are a little further out of town than the **Plough** and consist of a long, stone-and-brick range running along the street and containing ten tenements and a chapel. A tablet on the building records that it was built in 1665.

In 1837 the **Plough** and its land, consisting of three roods and three perches, was valued at £32 10s. However, this roadside

The old Plough

hostelry may have been there from a much earlier date and at one time could well have been the most westerly inn in the city.

The low, timber-framed building seen by the Royal Commission Inspectors must have been the freehold property that was put up for sale in 1928. The auctioneer's description fails to bring out any of the historic qualities of the building which ensured its entry in the *Royal Commission Inventory*:

'House built of brick and brick noggin with slated and tiled roof, containing:

'On the Ground Floor: Entrance lobby with tiled floor, bar parlour with tiled floor, comfortable bar, sitting room, kitchen and W.C.

'On the First Floor: Three bedrooms and a boxroom

'At the Rear is: a paved yard with urinal, W.C., pump and sink with water tap and a barn divided into beer cellar, garage and store room with lean-to-shed at end

'There is also a good garden and double doors and a side entrance from Plough Lane. Electric, Gas and Water are laid on.'

The main entrance led in from White Cross Street with an L-shaped bar to the rear and a smoke room with an enormous chimney-stack on the right. The large garden included an arbour and a summer house and was sheltered from the north winds by a skittle alley.

The **Plough** was bought by the Hereford and Tredegar Brewery and in 1938 they decided to demolish the old building and redevelop the site. The new building was typical of its period having a brick ground floor with stone reveals to the doors and windows and a mock half-timbered upper storey. Set back from both roads and with a large expanse of tarmac in front of the building, the building has little of the charm and attraction of its predecessor.

The **Plough** is now a solitary inn on the western side of Plough Lane, but in the mid-19th century it was balanced by the **Ox** on the opposite corner. It was from here that Thomas Williams moved to the **Red Lion** in 1842. The **Ox** was described as having one room downstairs and one room up and more resembled 'a salt-box than a house adapted as an Inn'. It was probably closed by the middle of the 19th century although the Ox Farm is mentioned in turn-of-the-century Directories and the Ox Farm Fish Bar (W.C. Bolt & Sons, props.) as recently as 1933.

The late nineteenth century Plough Lane was never a particularly busy road for it only led as far as Canon Moor Farm. Even so, apart from the **Ox** and the **Plough** at its entrance, the road had its own, well-hidden inn. This was the **Canon Moor Inn** or, as it is named in later Directories, the **Midland Railway Inn**. Its remote position was well-expressed in an article in the *Hereford Citizen and Bulletin* in 1955 'Until quite recently when the half-dozen almshouses were erected in memory of Alice Roberts, there seemed no other house in Plough Lane. Not until one had gone a considerable distance, past the allotments known as Aberystwyth Gardens, did one come to a cottage of good size, and on the bank of the Eign Brook. There was the old **Midland Tavern**, now a neat cottage. One doubts that it was a serious rival to the **Plough**, but passers-by going from the west part of the town, the Above Eign, to the Westfields, and also allotment workers would obviously use it.'

It was a simple beer-house and probably came into being to provide sustenance for the navvies who were working on the railway which was designed to connect Hereford with Brecon and mid-Wales. The first stages of what was described as the Hereford,

Hay-on-Wye & Brecon Railway were opened to Moorhampton in October 1862 and to Hay-on-Wye in July 1864. The line was eventually taken over by the Midland Railway in 1869 and it must have been then that the licensee started to think of a name change. Previously the inn had been known as the **Canon Moor**—its name was changed to the **Midland** in September 1876. The inn continued for almost half-a-century, but finally closed its doors in April 1913. Plough Lane now leads to an industrial estate and the pleasant country walk through Canon Moor Farm to Moor House and Widemarsh Common is but a memory.

Back into White Cross Road and a little further out from town is the **Buckingham House**, or just the **Buck** for short. It is one of the several public houses opened in the second half of the 19th century to serve the gradually-increasing White Cross development area and it was certainly there in 1862 when the landlord was John Ayland. Around the turn of the century the licensee was George Devonport, who also brewed his own beer, whilst from about 1935 until the 1950's it was William Woolhouse.

White Cross Road is connected to the parallel Westfaling Street (on one map shown charmingly as Australia Gardens Lane), which is the continuation of Barton Road, by several side streets including White Horse Street and Holmer Street. These two streets are connected by Cotterell Street, parallel to and a short distance to the north of White Cross Road. This is the home for two small 'street-corner' public houses—a rarity in Hereford. Nearest to the city is the **Britannia**, slightly larger than the surrounding houses and including a stone front, indicating that it was specially built as an inn. Further down the street is the end-of-terrace **Cotterell Arms**. Both of these inns were opened by 1885 and rather surprisingly, considering their proximity to each other and to the **Buckingham**, both have continued to serve local needs through to the present day.

White Cross Road continues westwards to a junction where Three Elms Road, leading towards Knighton, branches off to the right. The main thoroughfare, King's Acre Road, continues straight ahead towards Hay-on-Wye and Brecon. The White Cross, now rather incongruously placed in the middle of a roundabout, used to be by the side of the road junction. It was here, when the Black Death struck Hereford, that the country people, who were not suffering from the plague, brought their goods for sale, and where the afflicted townsfolk left their coins, doubtless suitably disinfected in vinegar, to pay for them.

A junction such as this should always have deserved a small wayside inn for the weary traveller. Surprisingly, this was not the case until the **Foxhunter** was granted its licence in April 1961. It was built by Rhymney Breweries Ltd. and opened a couple of years later in 1963. The **Foxhunter** was named after the famous show-jumper that was ridden by Colonel Harry Llewellyn at the Helsinki Olympics in 1952—the winner of the only gold medal won by Britain. For a while the inn was called the **Restoration** but it has once again become the **Foxhunter**.

Three Elms Road crosses the Yazor Brook and then climbs gently up the hill towards the Roman Road. Well-placed on the junction where Tillington Road, which leads towards Weobley, branches off to the left, and the main road continues straight ahead, is the **Three Elms Inn**. The whole of this area, between the King's Acre Road and the Three Elms Road is the Township of Huntington. The **Three Elms** was originally called the **Three Crosses**, presumably referring to the three roads which crossed in the vicinity—the Roman Road; the Knighton road; and the Tillington road which until recently crossed the Knighton road to run directly into Grandstand Road. This was presumably the licensed premises at Huntington, then called the **Three Elms Pool House**, that was offered for sale by auction in October 1920.

Back along Grandstand Road for a little distance to where a new pub, the **Cannybrook**, has recently opened. It is a typically modern inn and the site has no historic significance. Yazor Road returns us to the White Cross junction from where, along King's Acre Road, there was at one time two inns both within the Huntington Township boundary. The earliest was the **Coach & Horses** which was mentioned in 1817 when it was the venue for a cock-fight between the Gentlemen of the City and the Gentlemen of the County. It is not mentioned in any of the Directories and its precise location is uncertain.

However, the **Bay Horse** is still alive and kicking on the north side of King's Acre Road. This is an inn that is well hidden in the older street Directories, being listed under Huntington rather than as part of King's Acre Road. The earliest mention is in the will of Elizabeth Taylor which is dated the 24th November 1862. Her late husband, William, had a long lease on the **Horse and Groom** in Eign Street, but he also owned the freehold of the **Bay Horse** and the three cottages that adjoined it, including a wheelwright's shop, and Booth number 2 at the Racecourse. Elizabeth left her interest in the **Bay Horse** and the cottages first to her sister Margaret and then to Margaret's three children. In 1887, one of the children, William George Taylor, then an accountant in London, sold his share and that of his brother who had died, to his sister, Sarah Jane, for the princely sum of £300. Sarah had married Henry Welsh, a builder and contractor of the Phoenix Works in Commercial Road, Hereford, probably the same Henry who lived at Lyndhurst, just a short way past the **Bay Horse** on King's Acre Road.

In 1885 Mrs. Elizabeth Fox was landlady at the inn. She was followed by James Lane who kept the inn going over the turn of the century. This was still a typical small inn in the 1930's which was little different to a private house. The small, central entrance hall contained the staircase leading up to the first floor. One door on the left led into the smoke room and another on the right led into the bar. There was a small living room behind the bar and a large scullery at the rear. Drinks and food would be carried into the public rooms—there were no serving counters.

A long extension which was built along the front allowed the inn to be opened up with a larger bar and lounge, both served from a central area which had direct access to the kitchen. This was adequate until a couple of years ago when the building had another face lift. All the internal walls were removed to create a large open area with a new bar facing the main door. A large conservatory on the left has increased the available room making this one of the most popular inns in the neighbourhood of the city.

CHAPTER THIRTEEN

OUT TO THE RACECOURSE

The Inner Relief Road, although designed to follow the city defences, now creates a more effective break between the two parts of Widemarsh Street by day than the city gate was ever designed to do. On market days, pedestrians in large groups are now regulated by traffic lights whilst in the medieval period and even later, the traffic along Widemarsh Street was controlled by the Widemarsh Street Gate, where a toll could be charged for entry into the city. However, the gate could be closed for the night.

Widemarsh Street has been the main road leading from the city to the north, probably since the foundation of Hereford. From the gate it starts off purposefully enough, but as it approaches the railway it diverts to the west along Newtown Road and then takes up a more northerly course again with Holmer Road. The original course may well have been more direct leading through the Burcott, but the crossing of the 'wide-marsh' may well have produced difficulties from time to time. A second road ran from just outside the Eign Gate, on the western side of the walled town, to join the main road in Newtown Road. This was widened in the 1960's to become the Edgar Street section of the Relief Road.

Parallel and to the west of the southern part of Edgar Street is Portfield Street where a late nineteenth century estate of terraced houses developed. Halfway along Portfield Street on the corner with Richmond Street is the **Moorfield Inn** which opened during the third quarter of the 19th century. Plans to extend it along Richmond Street were proposed in 1939 but were shelved because of the war and the inn has remained a quiet end-of-terrace house ever since.

WILLIAM SIMPSON,

NEW CATTLE MARKET HOTEL, HEREFORD.

CHOICE WINES & SPIRITS CIGARS &c. GOOD STABLING

A large **CONCERT ROOM.** *Elegantly fitted up Suitable for Lectures or Soirees on reasonable terms.*

E. Hand & Son Birm.

Widemarsh Street without the Gate, as it is shown on Taylor's plan of 1757, always seems to have been well-endowed with inns and taverns. The late 19th century **Victoria Hotel** on the corner with Newmarket Street has already been described in chapter eleven. Just round the corner in Newmarket Street is the **Cattle Market Tavern**, often simply called the **Market Tavern**. In the late eighteenth and early nineteenth centuries the Cattle Market was held in Broad Street and the Sheep and Pig Market in the parallel Wroughtall, now Aubrey Street. Horses were sold outside St. Owen's Gate and there was a produce market in High Town, around and under the old Town Hall. The situation was far from satisfactory, but the City Council was not able to take any permanent action until the 'Hereford Improvement Act' of 1854. Timothy Curley produced a report on the suitability of the land to the northwest of the Town Ditch, which belonged to Charles Heather. Negotiations were rapidly concluded and the site was bought for £2,500. The purchase included the land, which is still the eastern part of the Cattle Market, and an acre of garden with a house that had been built in 1812. Progress was rapid with the new Cattle Market and in 1855 Curley told the City Council that 'Your new Cattle market will be equal to the greatest public improvement which this city has witnessed during the last 50 years'. For a short while Charles Heather's house was used as the Hereford Improvement Office, but by the time the cattle market was completed it had been opened as the **New Market Tavern**. By October, 1857, the Corporation had added to it 'a handsome room for the convenience of people attending the market' and six months later it was advertised as 'the Concert Room' at the **Cattle Market Tavern**. William Simpson was the first licensee and the new room, which is shown in his advertisement card to the west of the main building, is still part of the tavern.

Continuing along the western side of Widemarsh Street, there is now the City Council offices at Garrick House and a large multi-storey car park, but during the first half of this century an important building in this area was the Garrick Theatre built in 1882. It was here in 1916 that eight little girls, who were taking part in a concert to aid the troops, died in a fire. The Garrick was rebuilt after this tragedy and continued in use as a theatre until 1938. During the Second World War it was the Air Raid Post Headquarters and afterwards it became the County Library. Like all good theatres it had an inn next door—the **Royal George**. Indeed, the inn preceded the theatre, for it was certainly there before 1858, and it survived for quite a while afterwards, not closing its doors until July, 1957. Was this inn named after the ship which foundered at Spithead in 1782 with the loss of 800 lives, or was it yet another reference to George III—'Farmer George'—who reigned from 1760 to 1820?

On the opposite side of Widemarsh Street, on the corner with Catherine Street, is the **Old Harp Inn**. It was mentioned in 1826 and is shown, with quite considerable grounds, on the 1858 plan of the city. Was the name inspired by the union of England and Ireland in 1801? It was apparently quite well-established shortly after that date. Of course, it could be much earlier, for during the later medieval period, inns such as this, positioned just outside the city gate, would have catered for travellers who arrived too late to enter the city, or for those who wanted to stable their horses outside.

A plaque on the wall in Catherine Street, just underneath the first-floor chimney, records a major rebuilding of the inn with the initials W.P. and the date 1861. The initials are those of the licensee at the time, William Preece. He had been there for some time, for the *Hereford Times* of June 10th 1848 recorded the death of Sarah Ann, then his only child. By about 1873 he had been followed by George Pearman and his wife, another Sarah Ann. Sarah Ann outlived George and continued as licensee until 1929. She retired in that year having been at the inn for upwards of 56 years. When her husband was alive and for a little while later, the Pearmans had a second occupation, for they were also listed in the Directories as farmers. The 1917 Directory gives their second home as the Old Weir at Kenchester.

When Sarah Ann retired, the inn was offered for sale by auction on the 9th of April, 1929, by F.H. Sunderland & Co. The auctioneers remark, in the preamble to the sale details, that the inn is on the 'main Shrewsbury to South Wales road' and that they have 'much pleasure in submitting this very valuable property, the history of which dates back many years. Very few hotels have enjoyed such popularity over so long a period as the **Old Harp**, and situated in the centre of the city, close to the cattle market and the railway station, offers great possibilities for extensive catering'. At that time the ground floor had a bar, a lounge, a commercial room and a coffee room as well as kitchens, pantries and stores, whilst upstairs was the 'banqueting hall' and some seven bedrooms. Outside, around an open yard, were stabling for fifteen horses, a loose box, a coach house and the brew-house.

This was probably when the inn was bought by the Hereford & Tredegar Brewery, for in 1939 they put forward plans to alter the internal layout by joining the bar and lounge into one larger room. By this time the rather grand 'banqueting room' had become the 'club room'. In retrospect, it seems rather surprising that the **Old Harp** has managed to survive all the changes that have occurred in recent years in this part of Widemarsh Street. It also survived a recent change of ownership and is now a Banks's house.

The 1858 street Directory includes a mention of one inn in Catherine Street—the **Farriers Arm**s. It is not mentioned in earlier references, nor is it on the 1858 map or in the later Directories, so it must have had a short life.

Continuing out along Widemarsh Street and just past the attractive stone-built Coningsby's Hospital and the Blackfriars Monastic ruins, the **Oxford Arms** is slightly set back on the western side. It

is a two-storied, timber-framed building of seventeenth century date; the moulded bressumer is exposed, but the jettied front has been partly under-built. Inside, in the public rooms, are several moulded ceiling beams, but it is apparent that the building has had many alterations since it was built. Although it is some considerable distance from the centre of the city, it has been an inn for many years. In the *Hereford Journal* for the 17th February, 1780, there is offered for sale 'All that well-accustomed public house called the **Oxford Arms** with all brew-houses, stables, yards, gardens and land thereto belonging situate without W'marsh Gate within the liberties of the city'. A month later the *Journal* recorded that Joseph Partridge was to move from the **Black Boy**, in St. Martin's Street, to the **Oxford Arms**.

The **Oxford Arms** was number 42 Widemarsh Street and beyond it, at the turn of the century, were several terraces of small houses. Between numbers 52 and 53 was a covered driving-way that led to a track running through a large garden. The inquisitive traveller who followed this track would eventually have found number 52a Widemarsh Street—the **Pineapple Inn**. Founded before 1858, and named after what was then an exotic fruit, this was a brick-built, four-bedroomed house which included a smoke room and bar parlour in the front rooms. There was some stabling and a coach house across the garden. By 1885 a bowling alley had been built on one side of the main building, but this had been demolished by 1920.

A major problem occurred in April 1920 which is best told by the *Hereford Times* reporter of the day:

'Easter Monday incidents were responsible for the appearance of Charles Anthony Dallow, licensee of the Pineapple Inn, Widemarsh Street and Isaiah Bunney of Newbridge, South Wales, at Hereford City Police Courts on Thursday. Bunney was summoned for being found drunk on Dallow's licensed premises while Dallow himself was summoned for allowing Bunney to be drunk and for being drunk himself on his own licensed premises.

'T. A. Matthews prosecuted while the defendants were represented by J. Moore who pleaded guilty on behalf of Bunney and not guilty on behalf of Dallow. The police evidence was to the effect that the chief constable and detective-sergeant Hoskins were passing the Pineapple Inn on their way from the Hereford Racecourse at about 7.45p.m. when from what they observed they visited the Inn. In the bar they found the defendant Bunney helplessly drunk and two of his friends who were holding him up were trying to force soda-water down his throat. Dallow, who was in the bar, came outside at the request of the chief constable, and was asked what Bunney was doing drunk on the Premises. Dallow replied that he had not drunk on his premises but on the Racecourse; he was then noticed to be drunk. He staggered backward to a chair and his cap fell off. When told he was drunk he said "Me, drunk? Somebody will have something to say about that Mr. Chief". Evidence was also given by Inspector Smith in respect of Dallow's condition when they went to the Inn in regard to a gold watch and chain which had been lost in a fight on the green outside the Inn earlier.

'Evidence was given by Miss Margaret Dallow, daughter of the defendant, and by John Urquhart, who both said that Dallow was not drunk.

'The Chairman said they had not the slightest doubt about the case. They fined Bunney 10s. with 2 guineas costs, and Dallow was fined £5 with 3 guineas costs.'

This was really the end of the **Pineapple**, for the licence was not renewed and it closed shortly afterwards. Two months after the court case, the *Hereford Times* reported on an enquiry concerning the inn. The solicitors for the owners and lessees stated that 'while the non-renewal of the license was not opposed, they were not yet in a position to arrive at an agreement as regards compensation, as it would take time to go into the question of valuation'. The magistrates heard that the inn stood 50 yards from the street behind several dwellings, which made policing difficult and were informed that there were three other licensed premises within 300 yards.

One of these three inns was the **Essex Arms**, a short distance further out along Widemarsh Street but on the opposite side of the road. It had been built on land which originally belonged to the Knights of St. John of Jerusalem who had a cell next to the Blackfriars monastery. After the Dissolution of the Monasteries the whole area came into the possession of the Coningsby family of Hampton Court. The **Essex Arms** may well have been the cottage that was built by John Jones and his wife Katherine in 1660. It was a half-timbered building that was really only one storey high, although it had attic bedrooms. It was certainly in use as an inn by 1821 when James Tew was tenant.

The inn may well have been named after the ill-fated Earl of Essex who was a favourite of Queen Elizabeth. He eventually fell so far from favour that he was beheaded on Tower Hill in 1601. His titles of Earl of Essex and Viscount Hereford were eventually passed on to his son, Robert, by James I, when he ascended the throne.

The **Essex Arms** was just within the Widemarsh Turnpike, the gate at which turnpike tolls were collected. The tolls were finally abolished in the 1870's. The inn was offered for sale in July, 1930, when it was described as an exceedingly popular house that had, for many years, been in the possession of the vendors. Apparently the landlord, Charles Parry, had just died and his son had applied for a transfer licence whilst it was sold. The sale details described the public rooms as including the typical bar, bar parlour and smoke room, whilst in a lean-to at the rear was the kitchen, larder and cider cellar. There were two staircases giving access to four attic bedrooms. The grounds belonging to the inn extended to over an acre and some consideration was given to its suitability as a building site. Bidding started at £2,500 and steadily rose to £3,600 at which price the property was sold to Mr. A.J. Perrett of Stroud. He also bought some 5 acres of accommodation land at the rear, which the Parrys had also owned for £525. On the 12th August the surplus furniture belonging to the household was also sold. It

The Essex Arms before and after its move to Queenswood

included pig troughs, a fowl house, chicken coops etc. so the land-lord evidently kept livestock on part of his 5 acres, as well as using it for hay.

Alterations were made to the property from time to time but they were relatively minimal. For some time the field behind was the scene of the annual Bluecoat School sports day and the inn was popular with certain schoolmasters as well as having a thriving local trade. However, as time went by the surrounding houses were demolished and the area gradually became more industrialised. The inn finally closed to customers in May, 1969, and the grounds around it became the warehouse and stores for Hereford Timber. For many years the old inn stood by the side of the road with all its windows boarded up—a sad looking monument to a lost residential area of the city. Finally, planning approval and listed building consent were obtained for its demolition providing that it was re-erected on a new site. The new site was well outside the city, at the Queenswood Country Park, half-way between Hereford and Leominster. Work went on throughout 1989 and 1990 and eventually the restored building was opened to customers—as a café.

Widemarsh Street ends where Burcott Road leads off to the right, over the disused bridge which once belonged to the Hereford and Gloucester Canal, and the main Newtown Road continues ahead. Here, facing the junction, but actually in Newtown Road, is the **Race Horse Inn**. This is an old-established inn that was mentioned in the Directories by the middle of the 19th century. It was built on a site that was almost triangular in shape with the Widemarsh Brook forming the northern and western boundaries. Windows from the bar, lounge and bagatelle room overlooked a rockery that had been built on the bank of the stream.

This early **Race Horse** was a small, double-fronted, brick-built house which had had considerable additions built at the rear around a partly-covered yard. The cellar was oddly placed on the stream side of the building underneath the bagatelle room, and in 1917 the owner, Mr. Valentine, applied for permission to excavate and construct a new basement underneath most of the front building. Permission was granted and this considerable engineering task presumably took place. In October, 1930, Mrs. Mary Ann Valentine, the surviving owner and licensee of the **Racehorse Inn**, died and late in November the inn, together with the two dwelling houses adjoining, was offered for sale by auction. The furniture and other effects were sold shortly afterwards.

The whole property was bought by Messrs. Flower and Sons of Stratford on Avon and they eventually proceeded with an ambitious rebuilding project. When completed it was described as 'one of the most successful rebuildings' in the town's history.

The whole area was completely cleared and the new building occupied the site of the two adjoining houses as well as the old inn. It had a total frontage of some 135 feet. The foundation stone was laid by the then mayor, F. Wallcock, on October 25th, 1938, and a plaque above the dormer window has the completion date, 1939. The new building was apparently well received, to quote an enthusiastic writer in the *Hereford Citizen and Bulletin*:

'It is in the Georgian style, quiet and restrained in character, built in mellow red brick, with Portland stone dressings and entrance doorways and roofed with grey-green Westmorland slates. These materials blend beautifully, while the inside materials are of the very best. ... The accommodation provides a large public bar with oak-panelled walls and provided with built-in seating and darts recess, a gentlemens' smoke room and mixed smoke room, the former panelled in mahogany, the latter in obeche, and with upholstered seating so divided that each section will accommodate a small party of six or eight in one group'.

The new beer cellar was at ground floor level but was 'insulated and temperature controlled being lined with a thickness of cork'.

The **Race Horse** still survives on its corner site but now as the **Hereford Bull**. Unfortunately the mellow red brick has been recently covered in paint which quite spoils the original effect.

Until very recently there was an inn down Burcott Road, just before the low and narrow bridge which takes the railway over the road. This was the **Sawyers Rest**, first mentioned as **Burcott Row** in 1872 and again in the 1880's when it was called simply **The Rest**. During the first third of the twentieth century it was entered in Directories as solely the premises of a beer retailer, Reginald Matthews, for it did not have a spirit licence. The secret of its success was that Mr. Matthews brewed his own beer on the premises and by 1941 it was the only inn in Hereford, apart from the **Crown** on the other side of the river, where beer was still being brewed. It was during the 1950's that a full licence was eventually issued to the **Sawyers Rest** as a result of the surrender of the licence belonging to the **Raven** in Widemarsh Street, but this was not sufficient for as the area changed in character, the trade decreased. Although at one time it had somewhat of a reputation, because of its rather remote position, of providing drinks outside licensing hours, this was not sufficient for it to keep open and it has now joined the ranks of the closed and boarded-up inns in the city.

The **Newtown Inn** has been closed for some considerable time but the building has had little change. It is part of a small terrace on the north side of Newtown Road. From the latter part of the nineteenth century the end building was the Widemarsh sub-Post Office and the building next door was the **Newtown Inn** with double doors leading into the stable yard behind. When the inn finally closed the post office took over the building which it still occupies.

Across the road and now occupying the corner site alongside the widened Edgar Street, is the **Heart of Oak**. This is a relatively large three-storied building that is surrounded by modest two-storey houses. It was trading in the mid-19th century and was for sale in 1878 when it was described as 'a well-accustomed inn and public house ... with a detached brew-house and offices and a productive garden'. The inn contained a 'bar, bar parlour, sitting room, large club room, and six bedrooms', but even so, the far end of the building was a separate three-bedroomed dwelling house and shop with a detached bake-house. The inn was probably bought by John

Thomas who became the licensee. He was still there in the early 20th century and was followed by Thomas Owen Thomas, presumably a relative, for a Mrs. Sarah Jane Thomas followed him and continued there until 1930.

By that time it was owned by the Cheltenham Brewery Company and their Mr. Smith had a problem with the transfer of the licence. He asked for the transfer to be made to himself as a representative of the Company owning the premises. The Chairman of the Magistrates, Alderman Wallis, objected and stated that he wanted the licence to be transferred to the actual manager that the Company would install. Mr. Smith pleaded that what he proposed had been the custom for over 40 years, but the magistrate retorted that it was not the law. Eventually, the licence was granted, but in that instance only, and we can imagine that Mr. Smith left feeling rather hot under his collar!

The adjoining shop was eventually closed and is now included within the **Heart of Oak**. This large building now occupies what should be a prime corner site at the beginning of the Edgar Street section of the Inner Relief Road.

Just beyond the **Heart of Oak**, the turning on the left, which runs parallel with Edgar Street, is Millbrook Street. Down here was the **Millbrook Tavern** which was first entered in the Directories in 1891 and closed shortly before the Second World War. In 1901, a report in the *Hereford Times* was entitled 'A Risky Practical Joke':

'William Collard, gardener and George Collard, labourer, of 65 Millbrook St., were charged with having stolen a bottle of brandy, value 3s. 6d. from the Millbrook Tavern. Mrs. Parry said that at about a quarter to nine on Sunday night the defendants and another man called John Cole were in the Millbrook Tavern in the front bar standing against the counter. There was nobody else in the House as they had cleared out by half past eight. Cole ordered a pint of beer and she fetched it from the cellar. When she returned, William Collard was gone, Cole drank his beer and left also. While she was putting the glasses on the shelves she noticed a bottle of brandy was missing. She immediately went to Collard's house and accused the three men. George said "I have not seen the - - - - - brandy". She told him she held him responsible. Cole who was stood near said nothing. If they had paid she would have taken it no further but George threatened to break her head and used very bad language. She left. They were not drunk. When her husband returned, the defendants came across and asked if they were accused of taking the brandy, again using bad language. George took up a poker and threatened to break his head open if he accused him. A crowd gathered and William said outside "Yes we had the - - - - - brandy, and can pay for it or else they can lock us up". A bottle was then produced (broken) that was similar to the one taken.

'P.C.s Smith and Bird went to the Defendants house and found George laying on the floor helplessly drunk at 7.30 on Monday morning. When questioned, William said he knew nothing of the brandy, and also said "Look here, as I drop a corpse, I never touched the bottle!" George on being arrested also denied all knowledge of the brandy, saying he was drunk. However, when he returned home William led the officers to the back and said "Three of us drank the brandy here and threw the bottle down the garden". The bottle was later found.

'Mr. Wallis submitting that the case was for the County, remarked that instead of being ignorant illiterate men, had they been educated men in a different position of life and had taken a bottle off the Green Dragon shelf, the act would have been described as a practical joke.

'The Defendants had hitherto been of good character and had been locked up for 12 hours.

'The brandy was ordered to be paid for and each Defendant put 5s. in the Poor Box.'

Widemarsh Common is the large open area on the far side of the bridge which takes the road over the Brecon curve of the now-disused railway. There is a certain amount of confusion concerning the public houses in this area. The earliest mention is in 1774 when Arnold Barrell was landlord of the **Thatched House Tavern**. In April, 1835, it was recorded that 'On Sunday morning about 8 a.m. the dead body of a female was discovered in the pond near Widemarsh Mill. It was soon taken out and removed to the **Thatched Tavern** upon the Common'.

In December 1840, the death of Francis Jenkins, aged 71, for many years the landlord of the **Old Thatched Tavern**, was recorded. The inn was sold by auction towards the end of 1841 and the new owner changed its name to the **Cricketers Arms**, presumably because the game was played on the Common then, as it is now. However, this was not a popular name and by 1858 it had become the **Bull's Head** with C.E. Lane as landlord.

This is not the same **Bull's Head**, recently re-named the **Sportsman**, that exists today. The late 19th century **Bull's Head** or

Bull Inn, as it is shown on the 1858 plan, was on the corner of what is now Priory Place and Grandstand Road, looking across to the Common. The owner must have liked what he saw for he moved to an existing building on the eastern side of the Common close to the railway. By 1915 the **Bull's Head** belonged to Messrs. Arnold, Perrett & Co. of Wicwar in Gloucestershire. They built a flat-roofed extension to the ground-floor beer cellar on the south-east of the building and then, in 1929, extended the bar and smoke room on the opposite side of the building.

Round the corner from the original site of the **Bull Inn** and a little further up Grandstand Road is the **Golden Lion Inn**. First mentioned in the early 1870's, this inn belonged to the Hereford Brewery and was included in their 1898 sale. It contained the usual public rooms, four bedrooms and 'a good cellar in the basement' and was let to William Noden, who had been there for some time, at an annual rent of £18 10s.

Extensive alterations were carried out in 1938 when the adjoining house on the left was added to the premises. The wall between the two buildings, including the redundant staircase and chimney stack, was removed and a new stack added to the outside wall. The windows were then all altered to create a degree of symmetry. The main result was a vastly enlarged public bar and presumably an additional pair of rooms upstairs for the landlord. The **Golden Lion** is still in operation, now as a free house, and has given its name to the adjoining Close.

From the corner of Priory Place, Holmer Road continues up the hill past the Leisure Centre and the Racecourse. Just before the roundabout, where Holmer Road meets the Roman Road, and on the left-hand side is the **Starting Gate**. This is a relatively new development as an inn, the licence, which dates from September 1953, having been transferred from the **Castle Inn** in Stonebow Road. It was previously a house called Glenthorne. The main building is now a Beefeater House, but there is also an extensive hotel wing. The Roman Road, a short way above the **Starting Gate**, is the northern limit of the city.

CHAPTER FOURTEEN

THE STATION, AYLESTONE HILL & THE CANAL

Commercial Road, earlier Bye Street without the Gate, has an air of belonging to the commercial heart of the city, with its broad shop-lined pavements, even though it is outside the artificial boundary formed by the Inner Relief Road. Throughout the medieval period and until the end of the 18th century, much of the area to the south and east of Commercial Road was known as the Priory Portfields to distinguish them from the Portfields to the north-west of the city.

The Priory after which they were named was that of St. Guthlac, built around 1144 and occupying a large precinct on the south side of Commercial Road where the Bus Station and County Hospital now stand. The Priory was dissolved in 1539 and, although Sir John Price built a house on part of the site, the ruins were still suffi-ciently extensive in 1645 for Colonel Birch, in charge of the Parliamentarian troops, to hide some 150 men there during his successful attack on the city. At the end of the 18th century part of the site was used for the new County Gaol, designed by John Nash and, shortly after the Poor Law Act of 1834, a further part was used for the Hereford Union Workhouse. The latter still survives as the part of the County Hospital that faces onto Union Walk, but the gaol was demolished in 1930 with the exception of parts of the high perimeter wall and the Governor's House. The latter is now used as offices associated with the bus station and the old gaol site now includes the Classic Cinema as well as the bus station.

On the opposite side of Commercial Road to the Priory was Monksmoor Mill, which originally belonged to St. Guthlac's. This grew rapidly in the 19th century to become Herron & Sons, wool merchants, curriers and tanners. Next door was the Phoenix Works which included a sculptor, a builder and, for a time, the Stroud Brewery Company depot.

With such a variety of institutions and an extensive range of shops, it is not surprising that this main artery leading into the city should have attracted a considerable number of public houses throughout its history.

It was on the 5th March, 1777, that William Gough moved from the **Elephant & Castle** in High Town to the **Hop Pole**, which was then a coaching house with extensive stabling. Hops were first used to clarify and preserve beer in the latter part of the fifteenth century. Within a hundred years they were considered necessary for flavouring as well, and were being grown in quantity in Kent and Herefordshire. As hop gardens continued to increase, there was a great demand for coppice poles up which to grow the hops. Alder poles were considered to be the best and were some 16 feet high. The hops were tied to them with dried rushes or grass. Nowadays hops are grown on strings and wires and the hop poles are a thing of the past, only remembered in the occasional inn name.

In 1896, the **Hop Pole** was put up for sale as part of the estate of the late Mark Samuel Davies of Claremont House, Hunderton. Included in the sale were the four shops and houses on the city side of the inn and a complex of houses and other buildings in the yards behind the shops and inn. At the rear of the **Hop Pole** was Hop Pole Place and at the rear of the shops was Hop Bine Place. These were typical of the small courts found behind many street-frontage buildings in the 19th century and each contained four, one-up, one-down houses with small gardens, a wash house and a W.C. at the rear. The inn, which was occupied by the Tewkesbury Brewery Company with Joseph Jupp as landlord, contained a bar, bar parlour, tap and smoke room, as well as a market room and a dining room. In the rear yard, a newly-built stable block provided accommodation for 30 horses.

In March, 1903, the whole complex was again put up for sale, this time by the Hereford Society for Aiding the Industrious who had presumably bought it in 1896. It was offered as two lots, the inn, the adjoining house and the area behind on the one part, and

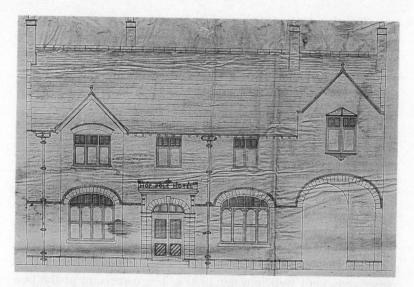

The architect's drawing for the front elevation of the proposed new Hop Pole building in 1903, as compared to the finished product with its more ornate gables

the other three houses/shops and their rear curtilages on the other. The second lot was sold to Messrs. Greenlands as a site for their proposed new furniture warehouse, but the first lot remained unsold. Two months later, the Society submitted plans for the complete rebuilding of the inn using both the original site and the site of the house next door.

The new building made provision for both sexes by having a separate 'women's entrance', which led from the new driving-way into the 'Women's Tea and Coffee Room' at the rear of the building. The Bar and the Smoking Room were both on the street frontage, the former being approached directly through the main doors, the latter from a central, rather dark hall. Upstairs were nine bedrooms, one bathroom and a W.C. Two years later, the four cottages at the rear were converted to become additional stabling, although Hop Bine Place continued to be used as houses behind Greenlands until well into the 1930's. The ownership of the new inn building was rather unusual. In 1905, and again in 1917 the **Hop Pole** is shown in Directories as belonging to the 'Herefordshire Public House Trust Limited'. By 1929 this had become 'The People's Refreshment House Association Ltd.' and continued as such into the 1950's. It has continued to be a popular pub up to the present day.

Almost opposite the **Hop Pole**, and on the corner of the well-named Monkmoor Street, was the **Great Western Inn**. In the earlier part of the 19th century this had been the Oddfellows Hall, but around 1863 the old hall was demolished and the site redeveloped by Charles Parry. The new building started its life as the **White Swan Inn**, perhaps taking its name directly from the **White Swan** in Broad Street that had just closed.

This was around the time that railway mania hit Hereford. Barr's Court Station, a short distance further out along Commercial Road, had been built as the terminus for the Shrewsbury & Hereford Railway. It had been opened to traffic since the 6th December, 1853, but it was not until 1863 that the line became jointly owned by the London & North Western Railway and the Great Western Railway. A year earlier, the Great Western Railway had also taken over the Hereford to Gloucester line from the local company. It would not have been long before the licensee of this **Swan** capitalised on the interest in railways and changed the name of his house to the **Great Western Inn**.

In the 1920's it was taken over by Mrs. Alice Baldwin who, having changed the name to the **Great Western Vaults**, stayed until well into the 1950's. After she left, the inn continued for a while longer but was eventually closed and is now The Palace, a fully-licensed Chinese Restaurant.

A short diversion up Monkmoor Street brings to light the **Nell Gwynne**, a substantial building on the corner with Catherine Street. This was, until very recently, the **British Oak**—at least the new name has a local connection! The corner site is shown as open ground on the 1858 map of the city although there were three small cottages in the area that eventually became the inn yard. By 1872 this three-storey inn had been built and opened and in 1907 permission was sought and granted to pull down the cottages and erect a stable block along Catherine Street, facing into the yard.

Miss Alice Pearce was licensee in the late 1920's and in July 1930 Richard Reginald Beaven applied for a transfer of the licence to himself. Alderman Wallis was again in the chair, and the *Hereford Times* recorded his comments; 'In answer to Ald. Wallis, Mr. Beaven stated that he was 30 years of age. He had been in charge of the Officers Mess of the Herefordshire Regiment for two years, and had been a warrant officer for seven years. Mr. Capel, speaking on Mr. Beaven's behalf, said he was a highly desirable applicant in every way, and a similar comment was made by Inspector A. Price on behalf of the police'. This was not sufficient for Alderman Wallis, who obviously thought that the **British Oak** was a den of iniquity. Although he granted the application he added 'I am sorry to see you going into this house. It is your choice, but as a young man, I would rather you kept to the timber trade, but perhaps that it not a thing for the magistrates'. Mr. Beaven stayed at the **British Oak** for some time, but had left by 1941—had he returned to his old regiment when war started?

From the Monkmoor Street junction it is only a few steps along Commercial Road to the arched entrance that leads into the disused St. Peter's burial ground. A few steps further and the **Merton Hotel** stands opposite the cinema. This shares its name with Merton Place, a terrace of small houses that ran at right angles to Commercial

Street in the 19th and early 20th centuries. The building, although present, was not shown as a public house on the 1858 map and was probably built as a private house. It was opened as a hotel about 1863 by Charles Farr.

FUNERALS FURNISHED.

THIS HEARSE WITH EITHER GLASS SIDES OR CARVED PANELS.

MERTON ✠ HOTEL

AND

General Posting House,

COMMERCIAL ROAD, HEREFORD,

(Within 5 minutes' walk of Railway Station.)

CHARLES FARR, Proprietor.

Saddle Horses, Dog Carts, Brakes, Flys, Landaus, Broughams, Private Carriages, &c., always on Hire by Day or Week. Loose Boxes & Lock-up Coach Houses.

MERTON OMNIBUS TO AND FROM THE RAILWAY STATION.

Hot and Cold Shower Baths always ready at the Hotel.

Apart from being the proprietor of the Hotel, General Posting House and Livery Stables, he also operated a funeral business. Farr died in the early 1890's and his wife continued to run the two businesses for a few years. By 1896, she decided to retire and the whole establishment was put up for sale by auction. Besides the hotel it included the nine cottages in Merton Place and the four houses between the **Merton** and St. Peter's Burial Ground. The hotel was described as containing: 'Entrance hall, bar, private bar, fine smoke rooms, coffee rooms, dining and drawing rooms'. There were twelve bedrooms and its status was assured by the provision of hot and cold shower baths at all times. At the rear of the hotel were two assembly rooms approached by a covered way from the main part of the building. The **Merton** was probably bought by Arnold, Perrett & Co., for in 1910 they applied for permission to build an Air Gun Club Room in the rear yard.

The houses next to the **Merton Hotel** and the cottages at the rear have long since disappeared. The hotel has expanded along the frontage and is now a Free House. Although opposite where the County Gaol used to stand, there is no evidence to show that it was associated with it in any way. A house for the Governor of the Gaol had been constructed in one corner of the Gaol compound by the

1880's; before that he had rooms within the Gaol's main building. However, there may have been a short period before Mr. Farr bought the building, when it was used to accommodate the Gaol Governor.

Continuing along Commercial Road towards the Railway Station, the last building to survive on the north side is the **Commercial Inn**. A very small building is shown here on the 1858 plan, but it was some years before it was opened as a hotel. The 1885 Ordnance Survey map shows an extended building with, behind it, the tanks and tan pits of Monkmoor Mills. By 1897 it belonged to Godsell & Sons of Stroud and they employed J. Fletcher Trew of Gloucester to carry out alterations and additions. He designed the rather flamboyant extension on the front of the original building with its ornate recessed doorway, and then inserted the large and impressive bay window on the first floor and a smaller one above it on the second. A year later, two additional bedrooms were built in the rear wing over the kitchen and scullery. The **Commercial** had a phase in the 1970's and 80's when it became the **Half Crown** after the pre-decimal coin which ceased to become legal tender in 1969. It has recently reverted to its original name and is all that much the better for it.

J. Fletcher Trew's exuberant front for the Commercial in 1897

The occasional diversion down a side street to find a well-hidden inn is still possible, but was much more practicable around the turn of the 20th century. One such house was the **Castle Inn** which was in what is now called Stonebow Road, but which was, in 1872, described as Slaughterhouse Road. The date when this first became an inn is not known, but it was mentioned in 1862 when Edward Morgan was the licensee. The inn was just across the road from the Hereford Corporation Slaughter Houses and it probably gained much of its trade from the men working there.

In 1952, it was included in a list of eighteen public houses and hotels in Hereford that were considered to be of special architectural interest. This was rather surprising for the Royal Commission, visiting it some 25 years earlier, had described it as modern. However, they did mention that the north wall was largely built of 13th century and later stonework and that in the garden was a large gable cross. The stonework and the cross may well have been the reason that it was called the **Castle Inn**, for there was never a castle in the area and the stones doubtless belonged to some of the buildings associated with St. Guthlac's priory. The inn continued in use until 1953 when the licence was surrendered to allow the **Starting Gate** in Holmer Road to open. The old **Castle** was then closed and the building demolished shortly afterwards.

The **Duke of Cumberland's Head** was described as being without Bysters Gate in 1777. At that time it was a well-established inn which was to be let together with 7 acres of tenable land, a large garden, a good stable, and a Smith Shop. Named after the Duke who overwhelmed the army led by Bonnie Prince Charlie at the Battle of Culloden Moor, near Inverness, in 1746, thus ending the Jacobite rebellion, this inn has been closed for many years and its precise position is unknown. The same can be said of the **Melbourne Arms**, supposed to be in Commercial Road in the 1860's. It would have been named after Viscount Melbourne, Prime Minister, with two short breaks, from 1834 to 1841.

The **Three Counties Hotel** was opened after the war at the top of Aylestone Hill on the corner with Folly Lane. It was granted an 'on licence' in February 1960, but this was not renewed in 1969. It was demolished several years ago and Carter Grove has now taken its place.

On the far side of Aylestone Hill, adjoining a small stream, and just inside the city boundary was yet another **Swan Inn**. Mentioned first in 1872, it continued to serve customers until a couple of years ago when it was closed. It has been boarded up ever since and although several suggestions have been put forward its future would seem to be uncertain.

A short distance westwards from the **Swan** as the bird would fly, but a little more difficult by road, is the **Bridge Inn**. This is halfway along the section of College Road which leads from the Royal

National College for the Blind to Roman Road. The **Bridge** backs up against the railway leading towards Leominster and Ledbury and is close to the bridge that takes College Road over the line. Across the road is Holmer Trading Estate which was where Goodwin & Hewitt Ltd. manufactured their encaustic and enamelled tiles. The works were started in 1884 and covered some 6 acres. The **Bridge Inn** had a license before that date—the building is certainly considerably older.

In the corner of the Trading Estate, just across the road from the inn, is the entrance to the Aylestone Tunnel on the Gloucester to Hereford Canal, now almost buried in rubbish. Although the canal had been opened to Ledbury by 1798, the cost at that time had exceeded the estimate for the whole length from Gloucester to Hereford. Work stopped and it was not until 1828, when Stephen Ballard was appointed 'clerk and engineer' that there was any enthusiasm for continuing the project. A new Act was obtained in 1839 and by February 1844 the canal had been opened to Withington. Work started on the Aylestone Hill Tunnel in January 1845 and 63 yards were dug in a fortnight. The Hereford basin was filled with water on the 22nd May 1845. The people who lived in the **Bridge** would have seen all this activity but may not have profited from it, for the building is not mentioned as a licensed premises until some time later. Although the canal may have been a source of some trade whilst the bargees awaited their turn to use the tunnel; the thirsty men who operated the kilns in the Victoria Tile Works would certainly have made much use of this well-placed inn.

CHAPTER FIFTEEN

TUPSLEY & THE OTHER EIGN

In a previous chapter, two inns which were actually just outside St. Owen's Gate were described. These were the **Sun**, which is on the northern side of the street just outside the city ditch line, and the long-demolished **Ship**, which was on the opposite side of the road, on the corner of St. Owen Street and Mill Street, and again on the edge of the ditch. The reason for this apparent anomaly is that both sites are between the defensive line and the Inner Relief Road. Before this new road was built Bath Street joined into St. Owen Street between the **Lamb** (as it was then) and the **Sun**—a street now called Harrison Street. A new road, which joined the main part of Bath Street to the eastern part of St. Owen Street, was built across one corner of the disused St. Owen's burial ground and it was close to here that the **Turk's Head Tavern** was once to be found.

It was in 1779 that this inn was sold at the **Nag's Head** in Broad Street. At that time the yearly rental was £3 13s. A few years later, in 1798, it was for sale again, but by that time it may not have been operating as an inn: 'To be sold by auction, situate without St. Owen's Gate in the Parish of St. Owen in the City of Hereford, Three Messuages or Tenements known by the name of "**The Old Turk's Head**"'. The tenements were on the eastern side of the burial ground, where Daws Road is now. The buildings, shown in a photograph taken around 1885, include the **Turk's Head** which by that time had become a common lodging-house. The buildings were all demolished around the turn of the century.

In 1858, the Ranters' Chapel was on the opposite side of St. Owen's Street to the **Turk's Head**. Following its closure as a

The Turk's Head buildings

chapel, there was a variety of uses including a period as the Salvation Army Barracks; a cinema called The Pavilion; a branch of the Hereford Co-operative and Industrial Society, and, recently, a Laundrette. A terrace of small houses, all with their frontages set well back from St. Owen Street, allowing small gardens between the buildings and the road, ran from there in an easterly direction and are shown on the 1858 plan of the city. Part of the terrace was demolished to make way for Weaver's Court, now St. Owen's Place, but a couple of the cottages remain and are used by Bullar's Printers.

Shortly after 1858, one of these small cottages, some twelve doors along from the chapel and in the middle of the terrace, became the **Bricklayers' Arms**. The basic two-up, two-down cottage with a side passage was not large enough for an inn, so a radical alteration took place. In the first instance the building was extended across the front garden right up to the pavement. To create a proper public house facade, the roof on the extension had to be higher than that on the original cottage, so the whole of that roof was raised to match. A single-storey extension, which included a kitchen and a brew-house, was then built on the rear and, at some time before 1886, a bowling alley was built at the far end of the remaining part of the rear garden.

The result was a long, narrow building with an equally long, narrow passage running all the way through the ground floor of the building on its western side. All the rooms opened off this passage, but those in the middle—the Parlour and the Living Room— because of the next door cottage which adjoined the flank wall, had no windows apart from those opening into the enclosed passage. The old front bedroom suffered from the same problem. All these rooms must have been impossibly dark and gloomy.

By 1901, the **Bricklayers' Arms** had been bought by the Alton Court Brewery Company and they also obtained the adjoining two cottages on the east. Once the nearer of the two cottages had been demolished, windows could be inserted into all the dark rooms of the inn. The interior of the building could then be re-organised. The plans produced at the time show a typical smoke room and bar, both opening off the side passage. However, there was one room which demonstrated a fundamental change in public house design in Hereford. Such a room, especially at the front of the building, had never been shown on any other public house plan of the period. It was a 'women's bar', with seats around the walls and a small bar counter, hardly the sort of change which one would have expected in an inn with a name such as the **Bricklayers' Arms**! All that separated this small room from the main, men's bar was a screen. A second front door provided separate access to the Jug and Bottle.

A later alteration made proper use of the additional height that had been gained in the older part of the building by inserting a second floor, again lit by windows in the side elevation. Eventually, the divisions between the various front bars were removed to create a large and relatively high public bar through the whole width and length of what had been the front extension.

A few years ago the **Bricklayers' Arms** had a radical face lift and became a 'theme pub'—the **Jolly Roger**—with a large bar designed to look like a pirate vessel. A brewery was installed at the rear and colourful pirates were painted on the outside flank walls, to the despair of the City Council Planning Department. Very recently the 'Jolly Roger' was hauled down, the pirates disappeared off the walls, and the inn, under new ownership, became the **Victory**.

A little further along St. Owen Street, the main road to Ledbury bears off to the left whilst Eign Road, the road leading towards Mordiford and Fownhope, continues straight ahead. Just before the junction, on the northern side, are Williams' and St. Giles' Almshouses, the latter dating to back to 1290.

Clive Street is the left-hand turning a little way along Eign Road. The **Belle Vue Hotel** was the corner building on the city side. It was built around the beginning of the third quarter of the 19th century alongside the other new developments that were taking place in this part of the city. Charles Phillips was the landlord in 1886 and continued to manage the establishment until the beginning of the 20th century. After this it became simply the **Belle Vue Inn** under which name it continued to serve customers until 1969 when it closed.

On the opposite side of Eign Road and a few yards further along is Bartonsham Road, a short street that joins Eign Road to the parallel section of Harold Street. The fish and chip shop which stands on the corner with Eign Road was, for many years, the **Barrack Tavern**. It was in 1890 that the Herefordshire Militia established their headquarters in Harold Street, at the opposite end of Bartonsham Road. The old headquarters building is now used as the County Record Office. Although the **Barrack Tavern** was in existence in the 1870's, it was not until July 1895 that the Hereford Brewery signed a ten year lease for the inn and the adjoining cottage. The rent for both was £28 per annum and in 1898 the Brewery let them to Mr. Charles Herring. The building was, as it is now, a long narrow property running along Bartonsham Road. The front, Eign Road, part was the inn, containing a bar, bar parlour and smoke room, while the one-up, one-down cottage which adjoined it, contained the kitchen. The inn was closed in the late 1930's.

A short diversion along Harold Street, in the direction of the city centre, finds the **Volunteer**, again very much associated with the Herefordshire Militia. Although it was mentioned in 1872, it first appears in the Directory in 1885 when Mrs. Leunette Meredith was licensee. Between then and 1891, she married again, for the Directory for that year records Mrs. Leunette Higgins. The inn, a Whitbread House, continues to provide a service to this large residential area, but is unlikely to serve many 'volunteers' nowadays!

There is still one public house in Eign Road which has not closed—the **Brewers Arms**, which is on the left-hand side just before the railway bridge. It is a detached house that may well have been built before the railway came. It was opened as an inn in the third quarter of the 19th century. In 1917 it belonged to Messrs. Godsell & Sons of Stroud, and in January Mr. Scobie, the active Clerk to the City Justices, wrote to inform them that the licensee, Frederick Charles Harding, had been convicted of 'knowingly selling beer, for consumption off the premises, to a person under the age of 14 years, to wit one Elizabeth Barber aged 13, the same not being sold in corked and sealed bottles'. One can picture the policeman stopping the poor Elizabeth, as she was staggering home with her jug of beer, to question her about her age. The licensee was eventually fined 10s. with 2s. 6d. costs. The **Brewers Arms** has successfully fought off all such problems and is running successfully as a free house.

Eign Road continues beyond the railway bridge, across the Eign Brook after which it is named, to where Old Eign Hill curves off to the left and Hampton Park Road continues straight ahead. The narrow and rather steep Old Eign Hill is the original main road—the present main road is a relatively recent improvement. At the bottom of Old Eign Hill is a single-storey, flat-roofed building that looks totally out-of-place. This is now used as the Brookfield Veterinary Hospital, but at an earlier date was one of Hereford's more interesting inns. This was the **Whalebone**, which was certainly serving customers at the beginning of the 19th century, and probably well before then.

The name seems to have changed with some regularity—in 1805 and again in 1811 it was the **Blade-bone**, but in 1826 and certainly by 1835 it had become the **Whalebone** with William Watkins as landlord. However, in April 1890, when the Licensing Justices transferred the licence from Ann Williams (deceased) to George Lane it was once again the **Bladebone**. Rather inevitably, the Directory for 1891 again refers to it as the **Whalebone Public House** with George Tringham as licensee.

Just across Eign Road from the inn was a narrow lane which led down to the Eign Wharf, a landing point for coal coming up the river and a public access point for people with boats using the River

The whale shoulderblade which was originally part of the frame of the doorway to the Whalebone

Wye. It must have been one of the boatmen, coming upstream with a barge from Chepstow, who brought the whale bones which adorned the entrance to the pub and gave it its name.

In August 1839, an auction sale was held at the **Whalebone** which included a 'useful team of wagon horses, implements, gates, hurdles etc.'—had the horses been used to pull barges up the Wye on the then relatively new tow path?

The **Whalebone** was a freehold property owned by the Hereford Brewery and was included in the 1898 sale. Described as being on the main road to Ross and Gloucester, it had all the usual rooms for a small public house. At that time George Tringham was paying a rent of £18 per annum. Compared with the rentals paid for other inns belonging to the Brewery, this amount was very small. It may well have reflected the gradual decline in trade due to the collapse of the barge traffic on the River Wye following the successive arrival of the tramway, the canal, and finally the railway. The **Whalebone** finally closed its doors on the 5th February 1956, but the licence was not lost—it was transferred to an adjoining house.

Demolition started and the unloved shoulder blade that had graced the doorway for many years was acquired by Mr. T. Stuart-Black Kelly. He held on to it for over thirty years, but eventually donated it to the Hereford City Museum where it is now one of the more unusual exhibits.

It is not uncommon for the Whale to be commemorated in pub names. Apart from the simple 'Whale Inn' there have been several called the 'Ship and Whale'. As whales' bones became more commonly available in the 19th century, the great jaw-bones, which could be up to 18 feet long, were erected as arches over doorways, often outside pubs.

The inn's licence was transferred to the adjoining house, the Steppes. This was a Georgian House that had been bought by the Hereford & Cheltenham Brewery. They converted it 'into a modern tastefully-furnished public house'. The *Hereford Times* concluded, rather hesitantly, that the 'builders have tried, quite successfully, not to destroy the character of the old house'. The new inn was opened as the **Salmon** five days after the **Whalebone** had closed .

Following a more recent comprehensive refurbishment, which included the removal of several interior walls and the addition of a large conservatory, the **Salmon** has become a very popular inn and appears well set to go into the 21st century.

A return has to be made back along Eign Road to the junction with the Ledbury Road. It was at this junction that St. Giles' Chapel extended diagonally out into the middle of the road creating an early but extreme traffic hazard. When the chapel was dismantled in 1927 and rebuilt a few doors further along St. Owen Street, the foundations of a 12th century round church belonging to the Knights' Templar were exposed underneath the later building.

Along Ledbury Road, beyond the railway bridge, the first right turn is Foley Street and here is the **Moss Cottage Inn**. This is shown in all the records and street Directories of the latter part of the 19th century as the premises of a 'beer retailer', for it is one of the few inns in Hereford that survived on a beer licence alone. It only obtained a full 'on licence' in February 1954.

In recent years it has been converted from a back street beer-house into a 'lounge bar and restaurant'. The change of status is apparent from the notice on one side of the door: 'Please Note: No Public Bar; No Pool Table; No Juke Box; No One Arm Bandit; No Dart Board: Sorry'. The opposing notice reminds customers that the inn is a free house and restaurant, but does recommend that visitors should 'Just come in for a Drink'—presumably also to meet 'Harry the Dog'?

Continuing along Ledbury Road, the junction with Bodenham Road and Hafod Road is now marked with a roundabout and just beyond it on the right is the **Rose and Crown**. An inn in the 1840's and probably for some considerable time earlier, it was described in 1862 as being in Scutmill Road, Tupsley. This is a reminder that the Ledbury Road was a 'new road' of the 18th century.

In the middle of the 19th century, William Stanton was the landlord. The **Rose and Crown** at that time was a small, Georgian, red-brick house to the west of the present building in the area that is now a car park. In front of the west door a very large peacock in yew, the pride of the landlord, led the way into a well-kept garden.

The old house failed to comply with the requirements of the age and in 1935 plans for a completely new building were put forward by the owners, the Cheltenham Original Brewery Company Ltd., and Arnold, Perrett and Company Ltd., who had amalgamated in 1924. The new building was opened in August 1936 in front of an invited audience including members of Hereford City Council, local magistrates, and representatives of the brewery. The senior magistrate, Mr. Oatfield, remarked that 'brewery companies . . were striking out in a line which the general public appreciated in providing really first-class houses where John Englishman and his wife could enjoy themselves in a reasonable manner in good surroundings. That was what had been done at the **Rose and Crown**'. Mr. Collier, for the brewery, made special mention of the architects, Messrs. Nicholson and Skriven, and the builders, Messrs. Beaven and Hodges.

The new building was described as a modern, picturesque structure, set well back from the road, which would be an asset to the rapidly-growing district. It was planned to serve afternoon teas and there were four letting bedrooms with hot and cold water, and a large bathroom. The public rooms comprised 'a spacious bar, a comfortable smoke room, and a charming lounge'. The latter, as the brewery director delicately put it, had been designed with a separate entrance so that 'ladies may take their menfolk for reasonable refreshment in pleasant surroundings'.

Mr. and Mrs. Thomas Chave had been the tenants since the early years of the 20th century and stayed with the new inn for a little while. However, by 1940, George Fry had taken over and shortly after he arrived he was involved in a 'scuffle' with a customer that ended up in court. Fry was summoned by John Herbert Watkins, a steel worker of Kingstone, for assault. Although there was an inevitable conflict of evidence, it would appear that Watkins and his friend John Davies, arriving at the inn near closing time, were supplied with two pints of bottled beer for which they were charged a shilling a pint. They complained and the landlord was quoted as saying 'Take it, leave it, or get out'. Watkins apparently said 'You can't put me out' and used foul language, calling the landlord 'a swine'. There was then a scuffle as the landlord attempted to eject Watkins. Fry got him to the door and Watkins was either pushed or fell, suffering extensive abrasions to his face and a sprained thumb to the extent that he was off work for 10 days. The case, which was held in front of the magistrates at the Hereford Police Court, was dismissed due to the conflicting evidence.

During the case, Mr. Symonds, appearing for Mr. Fry, reminded the magistrates that the **Rose and Crown** was not a common inn, so the landlord 'was not bound to serve refreshments to bona-fide travellers'. Moreover, he could charge what he liked for the drink he served and was entitled to turn out any person who was quarrelsome.

George Fry continued as the well-respected landlord of the **Rose and Crown** for many years. In 1964 he became Chairman of the Hereford and District Licensed Victuallers Association and in the same year was one of a party of 30 Hereford licensees and their wives who went on a week's 'working holiday' visiting Dutch breweries. This was not his first visit there—he had been captured at Ypres in May, 1915, when serving with the Monmouthshire Regiment, and spent three-and-a-half years in a German prisoner-of-war camp, finally being repatriated through Holland.

The **Rose and Crown** had a strange set of customers in 1964 when there was a dire need for an infant clinic in the Tupsley area. Mr. & Mrs. Fry agreed to open their smoke room as a waiting room for the toddlers, while the mobile clinic parked in the forecourt. For five years, on a voluntary basis, they supplied toys and comics to keep the children amused—as they rather regretfully said when their double life came to an end 'not many pubs can boast a smoke room full of bouncing babies on a Tuesday afternoon!'

The **Rose and Crown** hit the headlines of the local newspapers again in 1987 when the regulars formed an official complaints committee in an attempt to persuade the owners, Whitbreads, to give the by then very shabby inn a comprehensive facelift. After some picketing by the regulars, Whitbreads capitulated and agreed to spend some £150,000 on a major internal refurbishment. The work was completed in two months and the inn re-opened in April, 1988.

Further out along Ledbury Road, Whittern Way curves off to the left and some distance down there is the relatively modern **White House Inn** which was opened in December 1966 to serve the estate which was then growing rapidly in the area to the north of Folly Lane and Ledbury Road.

Tupsley was a township and is now a parish in the north-eastern part of Hereford. It was formed into a separate ecclesiastical parish in 1866 from part of the parish of Hampton Bishop and has its own church, St. Paul's. The old **Cock Inn** at Tupsley was apparently established as an inn in 1800. The name could derive from the inn hosting cock-fighting, or from the cock horse provided to pull laden wagons heading for market up the adjoining hill. However, Dunkling and Wright provide an alternative suggestion based on 'cock-ale'. This was apparently ale mixed with the jelly of a boiled cock and other ingredients. The authors do not make it obvious whether this drink was for pleasure or as a medicine!

According to Mr. & Mrs. Morris, who moved there shortly before the present **Cock** was built in the late 1960's, the original inn was in the building now known as Tupsley House on the opposite side of Tupsley Pitch. Mrs. Morris recalled the old 'Cock-road'—at one time one of the main routes into the city—which went through the back yard of Tupsley House. In the yard and close to the stable was the mill house where the horse-drawn cider press was housed. This was presumably the building which was offered for sale in 1835: 'All that old-established and desirable Inn called the **Cock at Tupsley**, with garden, malthouse, cider mill, cider house, stable, shed, piggeries, fold and about 3 acres of superior pasture land and orcharding adjoining, now in the occupation of William Teague'. The present **Cock of Tupsley** is just outside the city boundary.

CHAPTER SIXTEEN

SOUTH OF THE WYE

The old Wye bridge dates from about 1490, although parts of the foundations could be much earlier. It was built with a defensible gateway on the southern end similar to the one that still survives at Monmouth. The bridge's third arch was demolished as a protective measure during the Civil War siege in 1645, and afterwards was rebuilt to a different design. The gateway was also badly damaged, but even so it survived until 1782 when it was demolished as a consequence of the 1774 Act, being classified as a 'nuisance'. The bridge was widened on both sides in 1828 and, until the Greyfriars Bridge was built in 1967, had to take all the city traffic crossing the river and all the traffic travelling up and down the Welsh border.

South of the bridge is St. Martin's Street, which now curves to the west to meet the southern part of the Inner Relief Road just before the roundabout where the Ross and Abergavenny roads take their separate courses. Before the roundabout was built, this was a simple junction with a triangle of buildings between the two roads, joined at the base by the appropriately-named Cross Street. The roundabout and the approach road from the Greyfriars Bridge have taken up the whole of this triangular area.

Until relatively recently, St. Martin's Street had more than its fair share of inns and taverns, but as travelling habits have changed, the need for inns just outside the city gates has also diminished. However, one historic inn has survived, although with a recent change of name. Now called the **Lancaster**, this inn, which would have adjoined the bridge gatehouse, has been known for hundreds of years as the **Saracen's Head**.

The City Archives include a box containing 15 deeds relating to a messuage at Wye Bridge Gate which is noted as being afterwards called the **Saracen's Head**. They date from 1359, during the reign of Edward III, to 1526, when Henry VIII was on the throne. The inn is long and narrow and, until early this century, had a passage which ran down the eastern side leading to the river bank.

The various ranges of buildings and open yards, of which there are still many traces downstream of the inn, were the warehouses and coal wharves that were used by barges, or 'trows' as they were called, which transported heavy goods up and down the river from the 17th century and probably earlier. The trows continued to be used until the arrival of the horse-drawn tram in 1826. This brought coal from the South Wales collieries along the Brecon canal to Abergavenny, and then to the wharf just upstream of the Wye Bridge in trucks or 'trams' on an iron track. The opening of the tramway was celebrated with a public dinner held in the **City Arms Hotel**.

On the 26th January, 1796, the Minute Book of the Common Council records that 'A complaint having been made by several Barge Masters of their having been obstructed by Mr. Grundy, the occupier of the **Saracen's Head**, in passing their weirs [?] as usual, it is ordered that a Committee be appointed to examine into their complaint, and report their opinion thereon to this House'. Unfortunately, the report of the Committee is not included in the minutes so we do not know the extent of the obstruction. We do know that at that time the inn extended right up to the river bank. Once the wharves fell out of use the Corporation, who owned the building, dismantled the north and south walls of the inn and rebuilt them further back in order to provide the pathway which still leads directly along the river bank. They paid the tenant compensation of £100 whilst the work was in progress.

On the 27th June, 1840, Margaret, the wife of Thomas Protheroe of the **Saracen's Head**, died aged 72. Eighteen months later the unexpired part of the lease was offered for sale by auction. The property was described as: 'All that highly desirable and well accustomed Inn called The **Saracen's Head** with the Malt-house, Stables, and buildings thereunto belonging, most desirably situate at the south end of the Wye Bridge, in the Parish of St. Martin ... now in the occupation of Thomas Protheroe as yearly tenant.

In 1860 a case was brought at the Guildhall Court. The landlady of the **Saracen's Head** was being prosecuted for wasting water. It must have been rather ironic, for a few years earlier, before piped water arrived, she had only to sling a bucket out of the window into the river to get as much water as she wanted for free. The river has always been important to the inn, for in times of flood, the cellars can be inundated. It was during such a flood, in 1912/13, that the landlord hit on a new system to gain funds for the General Hospital charities. He charged all who came six pence a head to view a 'water otter' that was trapped in his cellar. It was, in fact, an old kettle which was suspended by a string from a ceiling beam. No one gave the game away and the well-reported exhibition, with Loch Ness monster overtones, went off with the best will in the world. The new name—the **Lancaster**—is not a reference to the duchy of Lancaster, but to the famous World War Two Lancaster bomber which is shown on the inn sign.

Just to the south of the inn Wye Street heads off eastwards towards Bishop's Meadow. On the opposite side of Wye Street to the inn is a car park. This open area is where St. Martin's Church stood until it was demolished after suffering serious damage in 1645 during the Civil War. All the plans of the city from that date onwards show this site remaining open, apparently waiting for a church that never arrived. The new church was eventually built in 1845 some distance further south along the Ross Road.

Next to the old church site was the **Duke's Head Inn**. It was doubtless named after the Duke of Norfolk, one time High Steward of the City, and was the first house in Norfolk Terrace. However, the present building is not in character or period with the rest of the terrace, being built in banded brickwork around the beginning of the 20th century. At that time permission had been obtained to build houses on the church site as well as reconstructing the inn, but apart from inserting chimney stacks and openings for fireplaces along the flank wall of the **Duke's Head**, nothing else was done. The present building must have replaced an earlier one, which was probably similar to the other buildings in the terrace, for the inn is recorded as early as 1826, when William Newman was licensee. It finally closed early in the second half of the 20th century.

The **Waterman's Arms** was on the west side of St. Martin's Street, to the south of a narrow passage called Waterman's Court and almost opposite the mid-point of Norfolk Terrace. It is not shown as an inn on the 1858 plan of the city, but its absence may be because it was a beer-house. It must have been there earlier than that date, for there is a reference to one Alfred Crompton, described as being 'of the **Waterman's Arms**', who died in December, 1848, aged 39. It was certainly functioning around the turn of the century, when John Carter was licensee, but the licence was not renewed in 1903. In 1954 the building was described as a shop which had some original ceiling beams dating back to the 17th century.

At various times before the latter part of the 19th century St. Martin's Street contained a **Talbot Inn**, recorded in 1826 with William Holsey as landlord, a **Race Stand Inn**, and a **Black Boy Inn**. The positions are uncertain, but the latter was not too far from St. Martin's Avenue. The **Express Tavern** was also in the St. Martin's area, somewhere near Drybridge, the large house opposite the end of St. Martin's Avenue.

The last building in St. Martin's Street on the east side is now a Banks's house with the rather unlikely name of the **Treacle Mine**.

The Treacle Mine

Until recently it was called the **Crown** and this may have been a later version of the **Roase & Crowne** mentioned in this area in 1661. However, there could be some confusion with the **Crown and Anchor**, described as being at Wye Bridge in 1858 but otherwise unknown.

The licensee of the **Crown** is described in the late 19th century and later Directories simply as a 'beer retailer', signifying its lowly status as a beer-house and this is confirmed by a plan of the period which shows the only public room to be the bar. In the early years of the present century it belonged to Showell's Brewery Company Ltd., of Langley, Birmingham and they carried out considerable internal improvements in 1921 and '22. Further alterations in 1926 created a little more room by moving the staircase and providing room behind the bar for the 'trams'—the heavy wooden supports for the beer barrels. The various efforts that they put into the building must not have had a sufficient success, for Showell's put the property up for sale by auction in July, 1930. It was then described as being 'thoroughly modernised and in excellent structural condition', whilst the accommodation was described as 'adequate'. Bidding started at £750 and it was eventually sold to the acquisitive A.J. Perrett of Stroud for £1,225. The Stroud Brewery must have given the licensee, Frank Waters, a relatively free hand, for as late as 1941 he was recorded as brewing his own beer. It was not until 1961 that the **Crown** became 'of age' and was granted a full 'on licence'. It was the last beer-house in Hereford.

A few doors below Drybridge House, on the opposite side of the road to the **Crown**, was the **Greyhound Dog**. This was the first house in Belmont Road, but has now been separated from St. Martin's Street by the Inner Relief Road. It is now standing in grand isolation but looking very much the worse for wear. Was this the **Dog Inn** where John Jones the Coroner held an inquest on the body of Walter Jones, Bargeman, in 1804? The verdict 'Died by visitation of God' leaves some food for thought. Or was it that **Dog Inn**, described as being 'newly-erected and commodious' and 'near the Wyebridge Gate', to which Edward Bigglestone moved from the **Ship** in 1848? The gate at that time could well have been the Tollgate which was close to the junction of the roads to Ross and Abergavenny. The **Greyhound Dog** was certainly the base for many of the horse-drawn coaches which covered the local routes, leaving the long-distance ones to the **Green Dragon**.

In the late 19th century, and for many years beforehand, there were two farms next to the **Greyhound Dog**, reflecting the rural nature of the part of Hereford to the south of the Wye. The first one was Causeway Farm, long since demolished but described by the Royal Commission as basically timber-framed with a brick re-facing to the front. The other was Pool Farm—a 15th century farm-house, now converted into several dwellings, which still exhibits much timber framing. The next building to Pool Farm was the **Pack Horse**, which was serving customers by 1858, when Francis Newman was landlord and, if the name is anything to go by, at a much earlier date. Pack horses, carrying heavy goods and travelling in trains, would have transported grain and wool into the Hereford markets from the upland areas to the south and west of the county, probably stopping at the inn to take refreshment and unload. It was a high, three-storey brick building that continued in use as an inn into the first decade of the 20th century, but its licence was not renewed in 1905 and it closed and was eventually demolished. The site is now at the corner of Belmont Road and Springfield Avenue.

Some distance further out on Belmont Road and just before the city boundary, which follows the Newton Brook, is the **Belmont Inn**. This is a relatively new inn which was opened as a public house on the 27th February, 1954 under the name of the **Newton House Inn**. The licence of the **Golden Lion** in Little Berrington Street was surrendered in favour of this new establishment. Newton House had originally been a gentleman's seat, but was converted to an inn to serve the growing development around Hunderton.

Hunderton was a small hamlet on the banks of the Wye which, for many years boasted a landing stage and a ferry across the Wye. It also had an inn, the **Vaga Tavern**, which has continued in use through to the present day. Dunkling and Wright suggest that this name is for Perino del Vaga (1500-47), an Italian painter who was a pupil of and assistant to Raphael. He painted chiefly historical and mythological subjects. However, according to John Price, in his *Historical Account of the City of Hereford*, the River Wye derives its name from the British 'Gwye' and its Latin equivalent 'Vaga', from 'its winding, and the beautiful irregularity of its course', and this is the more likely derivation of the name.

A short way down Ross Road, just past what was until recently Cross Street and facing the end of Hinton Road, is the **Ship Inn**. This is an old-established inn, for in 1802 there was offered for sale 'All that dwelling house, brewhouse, stable, and garden called or known by the sign of the **Ship** or **Plaisterers Arms**, late in the occupation of Thomas Williams and his under tenants'. The Worshipful Company of Plaisterers was formed in 1600, 'plaisterer' being an old form of 'plasterer'.

In 1898 it belonged to the Hereford Brewery and was described in the sale details as 'A Brick and Tiled House containing Bar, Tap Room, Private Parlour, Back Parlour and Club Room with three

Inside the Ship

208

bedrooms. The garden contained a Bowling Saloon, Piggery and a back entrance from Belmont Road. The rent was £35 per annum and it was let to John Cooper. The front rooms were small, with oversized bay windows opening into the tap room and bar. In 1936 the front part was entirely rebuilt and the rear part substantially reconstructed. The new **Ship** was much larger than its predecessor with substantial frontages to Ross Road and Cross Street. It is still a licensed premises.

A little further down Ross Road from the **Ship** there was apparently a **Victoria Arms**. It was said to be attached to Rees Terrace, but is not shown in any of the street Directories.

As the area south of the river developed with new housing estates, there was a need for new inns. Licenses were not simply issued—they had to be exchanged. A deal was struck in the case of the **Broad Leys** on the corner of Ross Road and Holme Lacy Road. Two inns in the city, the historic **White Horse**, at the corner of Union Street and Gaol Street, and the **White Hart** in Broad Street, had to close their doors to customers forever to allow the Cheltenham and Hereford Brewery to build this new establishment which was opened in 1938. The name **Broad Leys** refers to the extensive meadowland which was once such a feature of this area. The main entrance, which was on the diagonal wall, led into the bar on one side and the smoke room on the other. The side entry in Ross Road led into the 'Mixed smoke room'.

In the 18th and early 19th centuries Hinton Road was considerably more important than it is now and this is reflected in the number of inns. One, which was relatively well-established was the **Anchor and Can** at Putson. It has been suggested that the first part of the name could have been confused at one time with an 'anker' which is a measure of wine and spirits in Holland, Denmark, Sweden etc. and formerly in England, equivalent to eight and a third imperial gallons. It is also an old name for a cask which held that quantity. The 'Anker and Can' could thus refer to the means of storing and serving wines.

The inn was a brick-built house which stood practically in the middle of the old Hinton Road where it touches Holme Lacy Road. It was recorded during the first half of the 19th century, but disappeared some time after 1866. Somewhere in the same area, possibly nearer to the St. Martin's suburb, were the **Queen of Diamonds** and the **Dolphin** but their sites have been lost for many years.

One, slightly more modern establishment was a beerhouse called the **Loop Line Inn**. The two-mile long railway loop line was constructed around the south of Hereford to re-route the Newport and Abergavenny Railway line into Barrs Court Station. It was built in 1866 and went from Redhill Junction on the Newport line to Rotherwas Junction on the old Gloucester line. It now takes all the north-south traffic and is the only line to survive. The **Loop Line Inn** was probably opened to serve the navvies working on the line. It was roughly half-way along the loop itself in what was then Slade Lane but is now called Slade Gate. This road runs back from Ross Road as far as Bullingham Lane which it joins close to the railway bridge. The inn name had been painted on the semi-detached house in black paint and was visible until about 1950.

Holme Lacy Road has one inn within the city boundary—the **Gamecock**. The **Wye Hotel**, a little further along, is just outside the boundary. The **Gamecock** is on the junction where the Hoarwithy road bears off to the right, and has a similar history to the **Broad Leys**. Once again, two licences in the city had to be surrendered to provide the new licence. In this case they were the **Millbrook Tavern** in Millbrook Street and the **Plough** in Aubrey Street. The **Gamecock** was built in 1937, a little earlier than the **Broad Leys**, and had an imposing central entry which led into the Public Bar and the Saloon Bar. A side entry led through a childrens' shelter—they were not allowed inside the building—into a Ladies Room, whilst at the other side of the building there was the usual skittle alley.

Until recently, Hereford was more than plentifully supplied with licensed houses. In 1641 there were 63 inns and 154 ale-sellers. By 1825, this had declined to a total of 56 which included all the coaching inns. But by 1975, only 19 of those were still licensed and the number within the line of the city wall has now dropped to 15. This is, of course, partly reflected by an increase in the number of public houses in the suburbs and by an increase in the number of clubs, but even so, it is sad to see the old-established inns and taverns closed and boarded up. For, as shops shut their doors at the end of the afternoon, it is only the inns and taverns that are left to breathe a touch of life into the streets throughout the long evenings.

Sources & References

GENERAL WORKS
The Itinerary of John Leland, ed. L. Toulmin Smith, 5 vols., 1908
    (reprint 1964)
A Tour through the Whole Island of Great Britain, (Daniel Defoe),
    ed. P.N. Furbank and W.R. Owens, 1991
The Life of Samuel Johnson, James Boswell, 1791

THE CITY
An Historical Account of the City of Hereford, J. Price,1796
    (Facsimile, 1970)
Map of Hereford, T. Curley, 1858 (On wall in rear passage of Town
    Hall)
Ancient Customs of the City of Hereford, R. Johnson, 1868
Hereford in 1892, Illustrated, 1892
Outlines of Old and New Hereford, W. Collins, 1911
Modern Hereford, W. Collins, 1911
Historical Landmarks of Hereford, W. Collins, 1915 (Facsimile,
    1990)
An Inventory of the Historical Monuments in Herefordshire, Vol. 1,
    Royal Commission on Historical Monuments, 1931
The Inns of Herefordshire, H.P. Bulmer, c.1955
The Book of Hereford, J.W. and M. Tonkin, 1975
A Drink for its Time, M.B. Quinion, 1979
Yesterday's Town: Hereford, D. Whitehead, 1983
Hereford in Old Photographs, A. Sandford, 1987
Hereford Then and Now, Vols 1 and 2, D. Foxton, 1988 and 1991
Hops and Hop Picking, R. Filmer, 1982
Hereford and Worcester Railways Remembered, L. Oppitz, 1990

Alfred Watkins, A Herefordshire Man, R. Shoesmith, 1990
Ninety Years of Cinema in Hereford, (pamphlet) B. Hornsey, 1991
Hereford: History and Guide, R. Shoesmith, 1992
The Hereford and Gloucester Canal, D. Bick, 1994
The Transactions of the Woolhope Naturalists' Field Club, 1851 to
    date
Kelly's Directories of Herefordshire, Various years
Hereford & District Directory, Chamber of Commerce,1950-51,
Hereford Citizen and Bulletin
Hereford Journal
Hereford Times

INNS AND TAVERNS
The Old Inns of England, A.E. Richardson, 1948
A History of the English Public House, H.A. Monckton, 1969
Stories of Inns and their Signs, E. Delderfield, 1974
Pub Names of Britain, L. Dunkling and G. Wright, 1994